macromedia®
DREAMWEAVER
ULTRADEV™ 4
TRAINING FROM THE SOURCE

macromedia®
DREAMWEAVER
ULTRADEV™ 4
TRAINING FROM THE SOURCE

Nolan Hester

macromedia®
PRESS

Macromedia Dreamweaver UltraDev 4: Training from the Source

 Published by Macromedia Press, in association with Peachpit Press, a division of Pearson Education.

Macromedia Press
1249 Eighth Street
Berkeley, CA 94710
510/524-2178
510/524-2221 (fax)
Find us on the World Wide Web at:
http://www.peachpit.com
http://www.macromedia.com

Printed and bound in the United States of America

ISBN 0-201-72144-9

9 8 7 6 5 4 3 2 1

CREDITS

Author
Nolan Hester

Editor
Wendy Sharp

Production Coordinator
Kate Reber

Compositors
Rick Gordon, Emerald Valley Graphics
Debbie Roberti, Espresso Graphics

Indexer
Karin Arrigoni, Write Away

Cover Design
Steven Soshea, Macromedia, Inc.

Technical Review
Julie Thompson, Macromedia Dreamweaver UltraDev Product Manager
David Deming, Macromedia Dreamweaver UltraDev Product Manager
Chris Valiquet, Macromedia Dreamweaver Technical Support
Mike Barberelli, Macromedia Dreamweaver Technical Support

**This edition is based in part upon Learning from the Source materials
originally developed by:**
Stuart Harris, Judy Ziajka, Malinda McCain, and Jan Contestable

Thanks to everyone else who helped out in one way or another:
Tiffany Beltis from Macromedia, Marjorie Baer and Nancy Aldrich-Ruenzel of Peachpit Press,
and most especially my brother, Neil Hester, who guided me in the mysteries of Microsoft's
Windows 2000 Server.

As always, this book is dedicated to Mary (let op!).

table of contents

LESSON 4 ADDING DYNAMIC DATA　　　46

Making Text Dynamic
Making Images Dynamic
Adding a Live Object
Using the Live Data View
Making Form Objects Dynamic
Binding Menus and Lists to Data
Binding Check Boxes to Data
Binding Radio Buttons to Data
Binding Other HTML Attributes

LESSON 5 BUILDING MULTIRECORD RESULT PAGES　　　92

Copying a Recordset from Page to Page
Repeating Regions of a Page
Adding Navigation Buttons
Adding a Navigation Status Display
Linking a Results List to a Details Page

LESSON 6 BUILDING INSERT PAGES　　　116

Creating a New Recordset
Creating an Insert Page with a Live Object
Adding a Hidden Field
Using the Insert Page
Using and inspecting text input fields
Using Radio Buttons
Using Menus
Inserting the New Record
Checking the Form with Validation Behaviors
Linking to the Insert Page

LESSON 7 BUILDING UPDATE PAGES　　　148

Creating an Update Page
Building an Update Page with a Live Object
Adding an Update Link
Creating an Update Page Field by Field
Completing the Input Fields
Applying the Update Server Behavior

introduction

Macromedia's Dreamweaver UltraDev 4 combines Dreamweaver's ease-of-use with
the power of databases to create dynamically created Web pages. Think of the result
as Dreamweaver on steroids.

Macromedia Dreamweaver UltraDev extends Dreamweaver's renowned ease of use
into the realm of database-driven Web sites. If you already use Dreamweaver, you'll
feel right at home with UltraDev since the programs share many of the same
interface features.

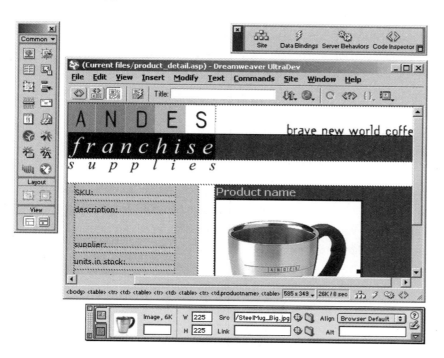

UltraDev's interface shares most of the basic elements found in Dreamweaver, including the Launcher, main toolbar, and panels. This Macromedia training program introduces you to the major features of Dreamweaver UltraDev 4 by guiding you step-by-step through creating database-linked Web pages. The book's 11 lessons start with setting up connections between your Web pages and databases and conclude with building server behaviors. This roughly 20-hour curriculum includes these lesson topics:

Lesson 1: UltraDev 4 Basics
Lesson 2: Configuring Your Web Site
Lesson 3: Setting Up Database Connectivity
Lesson 4: Adding Dynamic Data
Lesson 5: Building Multirecord Result Pages
Lesson 6: Building Insert Pages
Lesson 7: Building Update Pages
Lesson 8: Creating Searches with SQL Variables
Lesson 9: Displaying Server Objects
Lesson 10: Setting Passwords and Security
Lesson 11: Building Server Behaviors

Each lesson begins with an overview of its contents and what you can expect to learn. Lessons are divided into focused, bite-size tasks to build your UltraDev skills. Each lesson builds on what you've learned in previous lessons.

THE TRAINING FROM THE SOURCE APPROACH AND ITS ELEMENTS

Throughout the book, you will encounter some special features:

Tips: These highlight shortcuts for performing common tasks or ways you can use your new UltraDev skills to solve common problems.

Notes: These provide background information about a feature or task.

Italic terms: Words in italic indicate the exact names of files, text windows, tabs, or buttons within dialog boxes, and other items that you'll be using or selecting. The italics are meant to help you quickly find what's being discussed. An example: Click the *Select* button to navigate to the database you want to use.

Code font: Used to indicate scripts, SQL statements, HTML tag and attribute names, and literal text in examples. An example: Type `connAndes` as the name for your connection. Italicized code font indicates code items where you are expected to replace the italicized word with a word related to your own files or documents. An example: Type *yourConnection* as the name for your connection.

Menu commands and keyboard shortcuts: Other ways to execute UltraDev's mouse-based commands. Menu-based commands are shown as: Menu > Insert > Image. Keyboard-based shortcuts (when available) are shown in parentheses after the first step in which they can be used; a plus sign between the names of the keys means you press the keys simultaneously. For example: (Ctrl+Alt+I Windows, Option+Command+I Mac) means that to insert an image you should press the Ctrl and Alt and I keys at the same time if you're using a Windows machine or press the Option and Apple and I keys at the same time if you're on a Mac. Appendix A at the end of the book offers a quick-to-use chart of all of UltraDev's keyboard shortcuts.

SETTING UP THE LESSON FILES

You'll find all the files needed for these lessons on the accompanying CD, regardless of which of three server models you decide to use. The ASP folder contains lessons based on using Active Server Pages applications. The ColdFusion folder contains lessons based on using ColdFusion applications. The JSP folder contains lessons based on using JavaServer Pages applications. Whenever there's a substantial difference among the three, the book contains instructions for all three options.

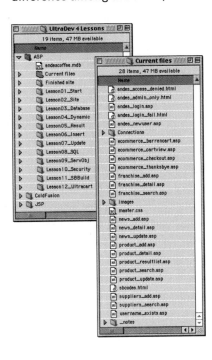

No matter which of the three folders you use, the structure within each is essentially the same: a folder for each of the 12 lessons, a Microsoft Access 2000 database file (andescoffee.mdb), and two more folders labeled Current files and Finished site. Feel free to copy the folder for your chosen server model (ASP, ColdFusion, or JSP) to your hard drive for faster performance. Be sure, however, to preserve the exact names and structure of the files within the Current files folder.

The files in Current files and in each of the 12 lesson folders are initially identical, but they will diverge as you work through the lessons. If you want to keep safety or in-progress copies of your own working files, you should keep them in the Current files folder and rename them in a way that will help you identify them. For more information on how to avoid any problems with the lesson files, see the ReadMe file on the CD.

WHAT YOU WILL LEARN
By the end of this book you will be able to:

- Configure your Web site and connect it to a database

- Add dynamic text, images, and form objects to your Web pages

- Build a results page for displaying database information, complete with navigation tools to display details

- Create an insert page for adding new information to your database from within a Web browser

- Create an update page for changing database records from within a Web browser

- Construct detailed queries for searching your database

- Set up passwords and security measures to control access to your database

- Add UltraDev's built-in server behaviors to extend the power of your Web site

- Build your own customized server behaviors

MINIMUM SYSTEM REQUIREMENTS

- Windows 95, 98, ME or 2000 Professional or Mac OS 8.6 or 9.x

- 64 MB available RAM

- 170 MB available disk space (Windows) or 130 MB available disk space (Macintosh)

- 166 MHz or faster Intel Pentium processor (or equivalent) or G3 or later processor recommended

- QuickTime 3.0 or later

- CD-ROM drive

- 256-color monitor with at least 800 × 600 pixel resolution

- Version 4 or later of Netscape Navigator or Internet Explorer (to view the Help system)

- Macromedia Shockwave 8 plug-in installed in your browser (to view the Help system's *Showme* movies)

- For Windows NT 4 users: Service Pack 5 or later installed

- Microsoft Data Access Components (MDAC) 2.1 or later (MDAC 2.1 is installed if you have installed Office 2000.)

- If you are using JDBC, a current version of a JVM, you need one of the following:

  - Sun's Java Runtime Environment (or the Java Development Kit) version 1.8 or later

  - Microsoft VM for Internet Explorer 5.01 (Build 3240, released 2/8/00)

  - Macintosh Runtime for Java (MRJ) 2.2 or later (with JDK 1.8 support)

- A JDBC driver for the database you'll be using

- Optionally: RmiJDBC—a client-server JDBC driver based on Java RMI

SERVER REQUIREMENTS

Dreamweaver UltraDev 4 supports the following servers for Active Server Pages applications (ASP):

- Microsoft IIS 3.0 or later (part of Windows NT Server and Windows 2000 Server)
- Microsoft Personal Web Server (part of Windows 95, 98, ME, and 2000 Professional)
- Chili!Soft ASP

Dreamweaver UltraDev 4 supports the following server for ColdFusion Markup Language (CFML):

- ColdFusion 4.0 or later

Dreamweaver UltraDev 4 supports any JavaServer Pages (JSP) 1.0-compliant server and has been tested with the following:

JSP servers:

- Allaire JRun 2.3.3
- IBM Websphere 2
- BEA WebLogic
- iPlanet Enterprise Server
- Apache Tomcat/Jakarta

Dreamweaver UltraDev 4 supports ActiveX Data Objects (ADO), Open Database Connectivity (ODBC), and Java Database Connectivity (JDBC) on Windows, and JDBC on the Macintosh. It has been tested with a variety of databases, though to follow this book's lessons, a Microsoft Access database driver is essential. For more information on building web applications, see Appendix B of the *Using Dreamweaver UltraDev 4* manual that came with your copy of UltraDev 4.

UltraDev 4 basics

LESSON 1

This book assumes you already know your way around Dreamweaver and are comfortable creating Web pages. UltraDev intentionally looks a lot like Dreamweaver. In fact, it has all of Dreamweaver's features and shares a nearly identical interface.

Unlike Dreamweaver, however, UltraDev contains extra features designed to make it easy to create database-driven Web pages. For example, the UltraDev toolbar contains one tool icon, Live Data View, that is not available in Dreamweaver. Similarly, the

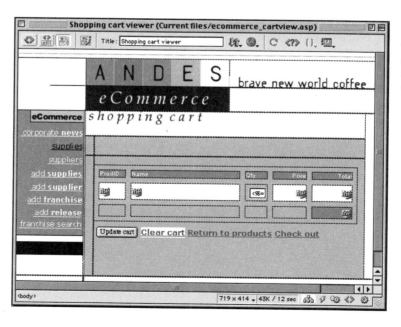

UltraDev's extra features enable you to build sophisticated e-commerce Web pages.

Launcher includes two buttons—Data Bindings and Server Behaviors—which open two panels unique to UltraDev. The Data Bindings and Server Behaviors panels will be used extensively throughout these lessons. If you have never used a database, don't worry. The book will walk you through the basic database concepts employed by UltraDev as you go.

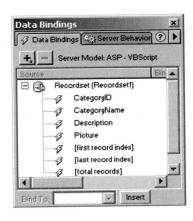 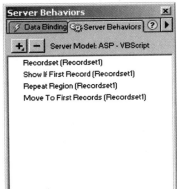

WHAT YOU WILL LEARN

In this lesson you will:

- Customize the UltraDev Launcher to suit your needs

- Set up your database driver

APPROXIMATE TIME

This lesson takes approximately 30 minutes to complete.

LESSON FILES

Media Files:

None

CUSTOMIZING ULTRADEV'S LAUNCHER

You can quickly open UltraDev's panels by clicking the buttons displayed by the Launcher. By default, your Launcher displays buttons for four panels: Site, Data Bindings, Server Behaviors, and Code Inspector. You can customize the Launcher to show up to 14 buttons, but more likely you will limit it to those for your most-used panels. Some panels, such as Data Bindings and Server Behaviors, share the same pane—enabling you to save a bit of screen space.

Customizing the Launcher by adding or removing icons is simple:

1) Choose Menu > Edit > Preferences from the main menu of the Site window or any document window.

You can also use Ctrl+U in Windows, Command+U on the Mac.

2) Select *Panels* in the *Category* window when the Preferences dialog box appears.

When the *Panels* choices appear on the right side of the Preferences dialog box, the *Show in Launcher* window lists the panels already appearing in the Launcher and Mini-Launcher.

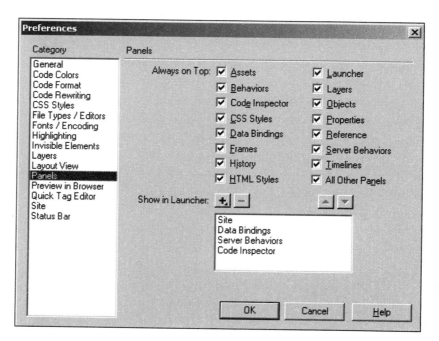

3) Click the + button to add a Launcher button, or the − button to remove a button, and make a choice from the drop-down menu.

Buttons already displayed in the Launcher will be dimmed in the drop-down menu. Once you release your cursor, the *Show in Launcher* list will be updated to reflect your choice.

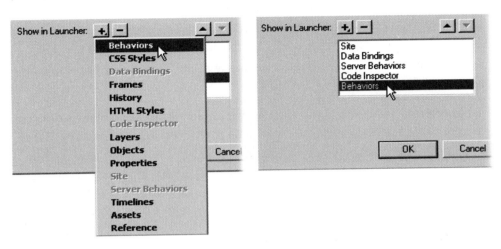

4) Click *OK* to close the Preferences dialog box once you've finished adding or removing buttons.

The Launcher will display the changes you've made.

SETTING UP YOUR WINDOWS APPLICATION SERVER

UltraDev can use a remote server reached via FTP, but in working through these lessons Windows users should use a local server—the Microsoft Internet Information Server (IIS). If you're using the ASP server model, you also can use Microsoft's Personal Web Server (PWS).

If you are using a Macintosh, or working with a mixed network of Macintosh and Windows machines, you should set up a single IIS server with individual directories and databases for each machine using UltraDev. This will enable individual users to upload files to the remote server and see their own changes in the database. Setting up Macs as UltraDev clients on a Windows server requires many more steps than getting a Windows client to work with a Windows server. For more information and help on connecting Macs to a Windows network, see Appendix B.

SETTING UP DATABASE DRIVERS AND ASSIGNING A DSN

In designing a database-driven set of Web pages (also known as a Web application), you often will work with a test database on your local machine or local network during development. However, the path to the live database on the final server may be entirely different. It may be on a different machine, and its path may be completely out of your control.

The Microsoft Windows resolution for this where's-the-database problem is to assign a kind of nickname to the database that will be good in all situations. As long as the nickname on the live data server is identical to the nickname on your local machine, UltraDev will be able to find the data regardless of the actual path to it. This nickname is known as the Data Source Name (DSN). For the book's lessons, you'll need a DSN for the included Microsoft Access database *andescoffee.mdb*. Assigning a DSN to a database is something entirely external to UltraDev—UltraDev does not even need to be running.

1) Click the Windows Start button and choose Settings > Control Panel.
(If you are using Windows 2000, choose Settings > Control Panel > Administrative Tools.) Users with Macintosh client machines need not do anything on the Mac but will be able to take advantage of this Windows DSN when connecting to the Windows-based database in Lesson 3.

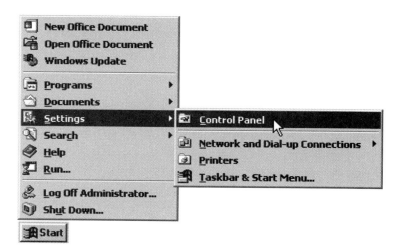

2) Double-click *Data Sources (ODBC)*.

3) Click the *System DSN* tab, then click *Add* in the ODBC Data Source Administrator dialog box.

Make sure you select the *System DSN* tab, not the default *User DSN* tab. If you create a user DSN, it won't be accessible to a Web server. Clicking *Add* will open the Create New Data Source dialog box, where you can select the necessary database driver.

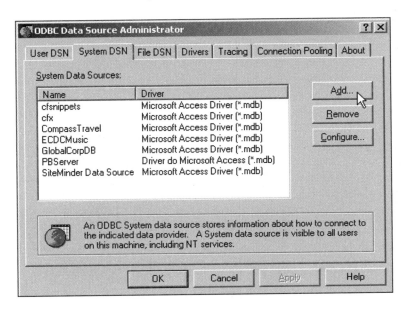

4) Select *Microsoft Access Driver (*.mdb)* in the scrolling window of the Create New Data Source dialog box, and click *Finish*.

The database driver is added to your system.

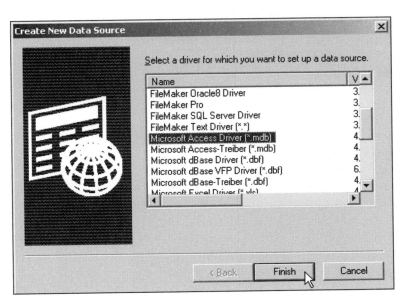

5) Enter andescoffee **into the** *Data Source Name* **text window of the ODBC Microsoft Access Setup dialog box. Now click** *Select*.

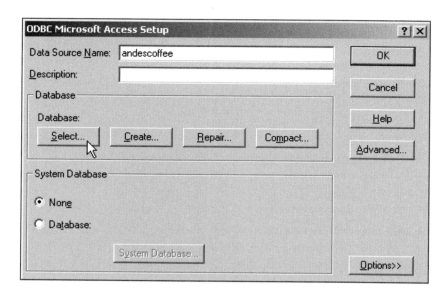

6) Use the Select Database dialog box to navigate to the *andescoffee.mdb* **Access database that you copied from the book's CD and click** *OK*.

The location of *andescoffee.mdb* depends on whether you are working from the CD or copied the book lessons to your hard drive. In either case, open the *UltraDev 4 Lessons* folder and look for the database in the *ASP*, *ColdFusion*, or *JSP* folder—depending on which server model you'll be using.

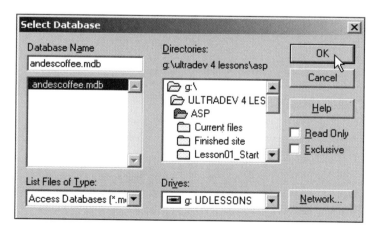

7) Click _OK_ again when the ODBC Data Sources Administrator dialog box reappears.

You're done adding the crucial driver for using the Access database. You've also created a shortcut for helping UltraDev find the database on your Windows server. However, UltraDev won't be able to see or use the database until you configure your site and create an actual connection to the database. Lesson 2 shows you how to configure your UltraDev Web site. Lesson 3 explains how to connect it to your database.

WHAT YOU HAVE LEARNED

In this lesson, you have:

* Customized the Launcher by selecting which of UltraDev's 14 panels you want to automatically appear (pages 10-11)
* Set up your database driver and assigned a Data Source Name (DSN) for use with the andescoffee database (pages 11-15)

configuring your web site

Like Dreamweaver, UltraDev organizes all of your projects as Web sites. Even if you want to work on a Web application that consists of a home page and nothing else, your project will have to exist within a site. The Site panel, which displays the directory trees for a site's local working directory and a remote directory on a server, makes it easy to move files between both locations.

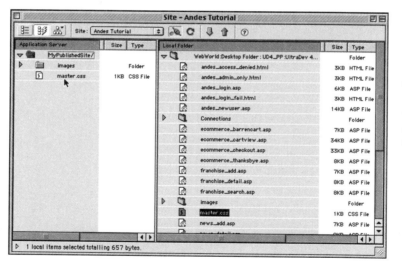

Once you define your local and remote Web sites, UltraDev's Site panel provides at-a-glance information for files in both locations.

Before you can configure UltraDev to move files from your local directory to a remote one, you need to have installed an application server that can double as a Web server. If you are running UltraDev on a Windows machine, you have two options: installing Microsoft Personal Web Server (PSW) on that same machine or connecting to a Windows NT or 2000 server running Microsoft Internet Information Server (IIS) 3.0 or later. (For more information, see Appendix B.)

If you are using UltraDev on a Mac, your only option is to connect to a Unix server, or a Windows NT or 2000 Server running IIS. Compared to a Windows-only set up, connecting a Mac client to a Windows server takes some extra steps. If you have not already done so, follow the instructions in Appendix B: Connecting Macintoshes to a Windows Server.

WHAT YOU WILL LEARN

In this lesson, you will:

- Define a new Web site within Macromedia Dreamweaver UltraDev
- Move files on your local computer to your remote Web site

APPROXIMATE TIME
This lesson takes approximately 45 minutes to complete.

LESSON FILES
Media Files:
None

Beginning Files:
All the files within the folder \UltraDev 4 Lessons\...\Current files

Completed Files:
Same as Beginning Files

DEFINING YOUR WEB SITE

If you closed UltraDev to set up your database driver in Lesson 1, start it again. When you do, you'll probably be looking at an unnamed blank window.

You'll start by defining a new site called Andes Tutorial.

1) Choose Site > New Site or choose *Define Sites* from the Site panel's *Site* drop-down menu and click *New* when the Define Sites dialog box appears.

If the Site panel isn't already visible, just click its icon in the Launcher or Mini-Launcher. The Define Sites dialog box, when it appears, will list any other sites you've already created in UltraDev or Dreamweaver—even an old version of Dreamweaver.

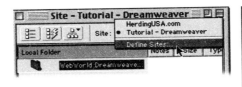
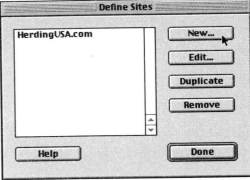

2) Select *Local Info* in the *Category* window when the Site Definition dialog box appears, then type Andes Tutorial **into the *Site Name* text window.**

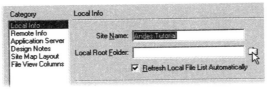
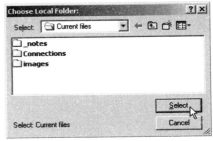

3) Click the folder icon on the right side of the *Local Root Folder* text window and browse to where you have stored your UltraDev 4 Lessons folder. Once you navigate down to: ...\UltraDev 4 Lessons\ASP\Current Files\ click *Select* (Windows) or *Choose* (Macintosh) to choose *Current Files* as your root folder.

If you are using the JSP server model, navigate instead to: ...\UltraDev 4 Lessons\ JSP\Current Files\. With ColdFusion, navigate to: ...\UltraDev 4 Lessons\ ColdFusion\Current Files\.

4) Be sure the *Refresh Local File List Automatically* and *Enable Cache* boxes are checked when the Site Definition dialog box reappears.

You can leave the *HTTP Address* text field blank.

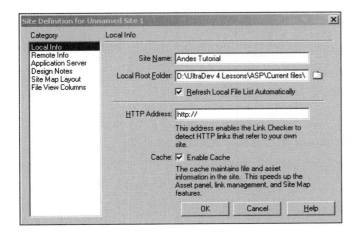

5) Select *Remote Info* in the *Category* window, and use the *Access* drop-down menu to select *Local/Network* or *FTP*.

The *Local/Network* connection will be a bit faster than FTP. If you are on a Mac, however, the *Local/Network* approach also requires that AppleTalk and File Services for Macintosh be installed on the Windows NT or 2000 server. For more information, see Appendix B.

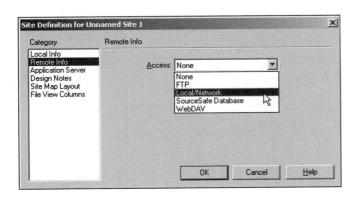

19

6) If you chose *Local/Network* in step 5, click the *Remote Folder* icon to browse to: C:\Inetpub\wwwroot. Create a new folder named andes_extranet **inside the wwwroot folder. The complete path will be C:\Inetpub \wwwroot \andes_extranet.**

Be sure to check *Refresh Remote File List Automatically* but leave the *Check In/Out* box blank.

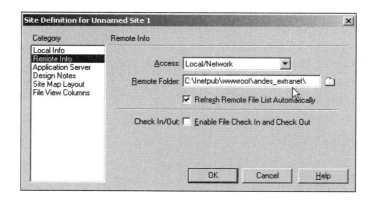

7) If you chose *FTP* in step 5, enter the Windows server's IP address in the *FTP Host* field—regardless of whether your local machine is Windows or Mac.

Unless you do it ahead of time, you'll need to switch to the Windows server and create a new folder named *MyPublishedSite* inside the *wwwroot* folder. After that's done, type *MyPublishedSite/* into the *Host Directory* window and enter a *Login* (user name) and *Password*. (The *Login* and *Password* must be created on the Windows server before the Windows or Mac client can open the *MyPublishedSite* folder.) Be sure to check *Save* but leave the *Check In/Out* box blank.

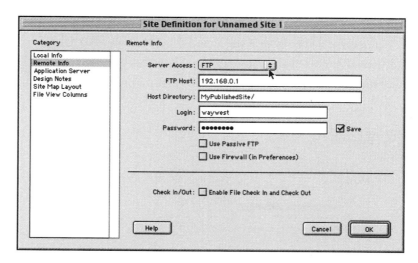

20

NOTE *The Check In/Out feature is not used in this book. However, it's a crucial feature when working on a site with other people since it keeps you from overwriting each other's work on the server. Checking out a file reserves it for your exclusive use until you check it back into the system. A read-only copy of the file is left on the server while the file is checked out.*

8) Select *Application Server* in the *Category* window, then use the drop-down menus to select settings appropriate for your server type. Your choices are:

Server Model: *ASP 2.0, JSP 1.0,* or *ColdFusion 4.0*

Default Scripting Language: *If using ASP, VBScript or JavaScript. If using JSP or ColdFusion, the default scripting language will be set for you.*

Page Extension: *.asp, .jsp or .cfm*

URL Prefix (if using Local/Network): *http://localhost/andes_extranet/*

URL Prefix (if using FTP): *http://[your server's IP address]/MyPublishedSite/*

The *Access, Remote Folder,* and *Refresh Remote File List Automatically* options will automatically use the same defaults as the *Remote Info* category. In some cases, the application server and the remote server may be different. The URL will be used when you preview your pages in a Web browser after transferring them to the server. It's also used when you select the Live Data View mode (see Lesson 4). The URL prefix must end with a forward slash.

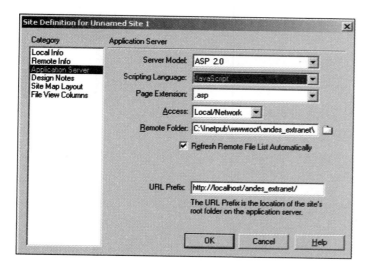

9) Skip the *Design Notes* category and in the *Site Map Layout* category, define the site's *Home Page* by using the folder icon to navigate to: ...\UltraDev 4 Lessons\ASP\Current Files\product_search. Once you reach the file, click *Open* (*Choose* on the Mac) to select it as the home page.

If you're using JSP, the file path would be: ...\JSP\Current Files\product_search.asp. If you're using ColdFusion, the file path would be: ...\ColdFusion\Current Files\ product_search.asp.

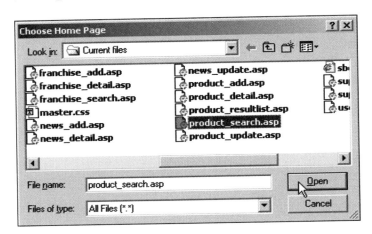

10) Click *OK* when the Site Definition dialog box reappears, then click *Done* to close the Define Sites dialog box.

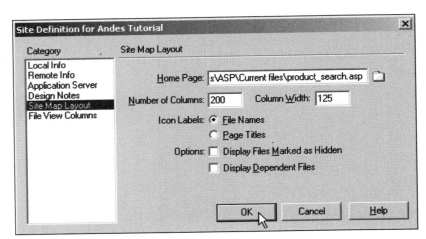

11) Click *OK* when the dialog box appears offering to create a cache for the site.

The Andes Tutorial site will open in the Site palette, with the *Local Folder* directory in the right pane. To see the empty *Remote Site* server pane on the left, click the Site panel's bottom-left arrow. You are now ready to transfer files from your local folder to the server, as explained in the next task.

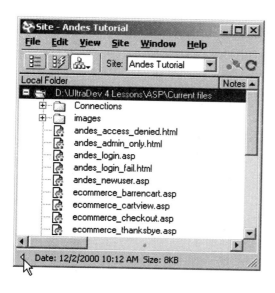

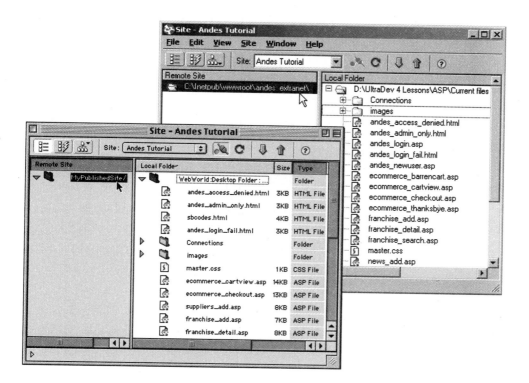

TRANSFERRING LOCAL FILES TO THE REMOTE SITE

Transferring the entire Andes Tutorial site to the server is not particularly desirable (although you could, by selecting the top line in the *Local Folder* pane and clicking the *Put* button). It is, however, a good idea to transfer all the images you will need on the server. Here's how to transfer the image files:

1) Open the Andes Tutorial site if it's not already open and bring the Site panel to the foreground by clicking its icon in the Launcher.

To expand the Site panel to show the Local Folder and the Remote Site, click the panel's bottom-left arrow.

2) Select the *images* folder in the *Local Folder* pane and click the *Put File(s)* button (the up arrow) on the Site panel toolbar.

The entire subfolder of images—including, in this case, the *product_images* folder and its contents—is copied to the Remote Folder in their correct relationship.

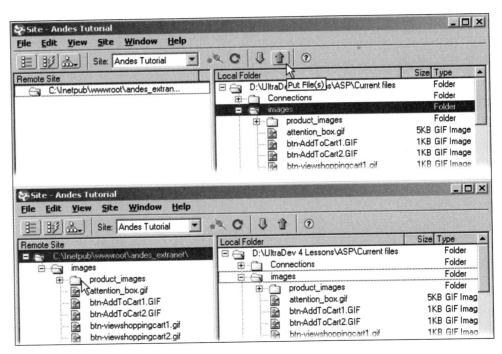

3) Select the CSS style sheet file *master.css* in the *Local Folder* pane and click the *Put* button again.

The file is also added to the *Remote Site* pane.

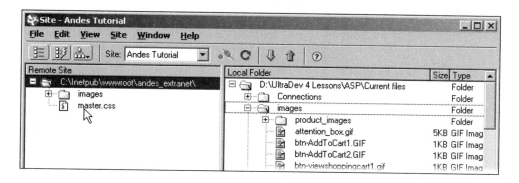

4) In the Site's *Local Folder* pane, double-click *product_detail* to take a look at the site's home page.

From the design point of view, this is pretty much a finished page. What it lacks—and what you are going to add in the next lesson—is actual product information from the Access database, *andescoffee.mdb*.

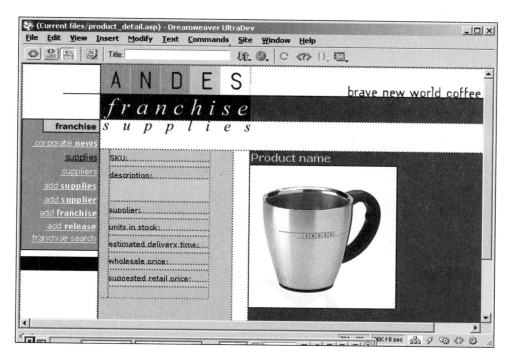

25

TIP *Generally, you'll use the Site panel to transfer individual files to the server. However, you also can transfer open files by clicking the toolbar's File Management button, which displays a combined up-and-down arrow.*

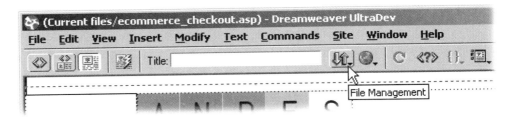

WHAT YOU HAVE LEARNED

In this lesson you have:

- Defined a local root directory for your UltraDev Web site and enabled a cache for the files (pages 18–19)

- Defined a remote directory for your UltraDev Web site and configured a local network or FTP connection (pages 19–20)

- Established ASP, JSP, or ColdFusion as your application server model for working with UltraDev's remote Web site (page 21)

- Used UltraDev's Put feature to move files and folders from your local Web directory to your remote Web site (pages 24–26)

setting up database connectivity

LESSON 3

Even though you set up a DSN for the Andes Coffee database, it is not yet available for use on your Web pages. After all, your computer may have definitions of 100 DSNs, but the Andes extranet has no interest whatsoever in 99 of them. The process of bringing live data to your Macromedia Dreamweaver UltraDev pages begins with the creation of a data connection, which becomes a property of the site in which you created it. You'll establish a data connection in the following exercise. You'll need to use a menu option on one of the site files—so if you closed all the Andes Tutorial site files at the end of the previous lesson, reopen one now.

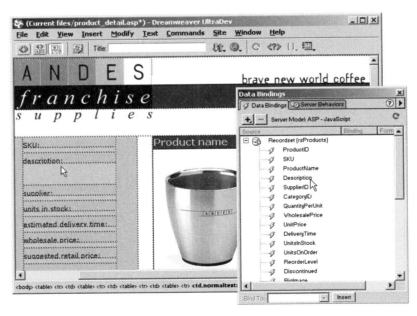

The recordset created in this lesson will enable you to start filling the product detail page with database information.

The procedure for establishing a database connection varies according to your server technology. An ASP application server can directly access the ODBC DSN you created in Lesson 2, making it the most straightforward type of connection. Theoretically, a JSP server cannot access an ODBC data source, but if the correct Java Runtime Environment (JRE) is running, a special driver class can be invoked to make the connection. If ColdFusion is your server technology, you'll need to register the Andes Coffee database as a ColdFusion data source, in the ColdFusion server administrator.

WHAT YOU WILL LEARN

In this lesson, you will:

- Establish a connection between your UltraDev site and the database you'll be using for the rest of the book

- Define the database connection based on the server technology you are using

- Add a recordset to a particular page in your site by building a database query statement

APPROXIMATE TIME

This lesson takes approximately one hour to complete.

LESSON FILES

Media Files:

None

Beginning Files:

\UltraDev 4 Lessons\...\Current files\product_detail

Completed Files:

Same as Beginning Files

DEFINING A DATABASE CONNECTION FOR ASP

The database connection acts as the pipeline that connects your UltraDev pages to your database. In effect, it acts as a pointer for communication between the two. You'll only have to define one connection for most sites. In this exercise, you'll learn how to define a database connection for ASP.

1) Open the Andes Tutorial site and choose Modify > Connections.

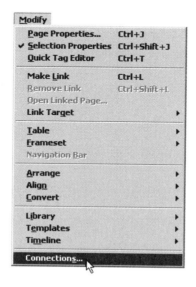

The Connections dialog box appears.

2) In the Connections dialog box, click *New* and select *Data Source Name (DSN)* from the drop-down menu.

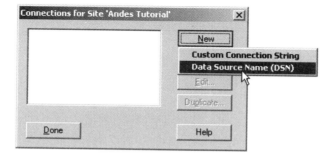

The Data Source Name dialog box appears.

3) Type connAndes in the *Connection Name* text field.

Spaces cannot be used in connection names, and you cannot edit the names later.

4) In the Data Source Name (DSN) drop-down menu, select *andescoffee*, the DSN you created in Lesson 1.

The drop-down menu will show all the DSNs on your system, though not in alphabetical order. Leave the *User Name* and *Password* text fields blank. (Both fields are sometimes necessary because some DSNs may be password-protected. However, the DSN you are using for this tutorial is unprotected.) Leave *UltraDev Should Connect* set to the default *Using Local DSN*.

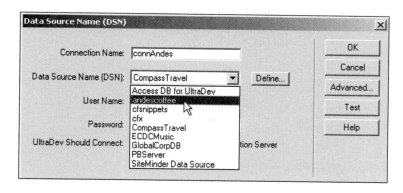

TIP *On the Macintosh, you cannot use the DSN drop-down menu. Instead, type into the text field the exact name of the DSN as originally created on the Windows server. In this case, that would be* andescoffee.

5) Test the database connection by clicking *Test*. Unless there's a problem with the system resources, you will see the message "Connection was made successfully." Click *OK* to close the message box.

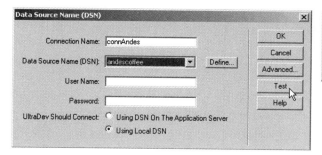

The Data Source Name dialog box will reappear.

6) Click *OK* in the Data Source Name dialog box. Click *Done* to close the Connections dialog box.

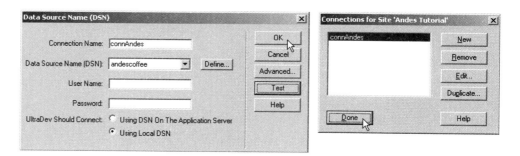

DEFINING A DATABASE CONNECTION FOR JSP

The database connection acts as the pipeline that connects your UltraDev pages to your database. In effect, it acts as a pointer for communication between the two and you'll only have to define one connection for most sites. In this exercise, you'll learn how to define a database connection using JSP.

1) Open the Andes Tutorial site and choose Modify > Connections.

The Connections dialog box appears.

2) Click *New* and select *ODBC Database (Sun JDBC-ODBC Driver)* from the drop-down menu.

The Data Source Name dialog box appears.

3) Type connAndes in the *Connection Name* text window.

Spaces cannot be used in connection names, and you cannot edit the names later.

4) In the Driver text window, type the default driver class:

sun.jdbc.odbc.JdbcOdbcDriver. **In the URL text window, replace the** [database] **token with the DSN name, in this case making the complete URL string** *jdbc:odbc:andescoffee.*

Leave the *User Name* and *Password* text windows blank. Leave *UltraDev Should Connect* set to the default *Using Driver On This Machine.*

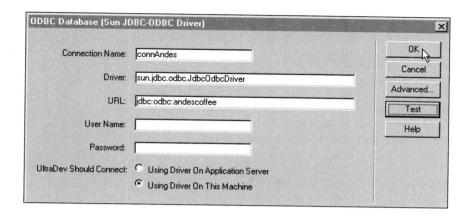

5) Test the database connection by clicking *Test*. Unless there's a problem with the system resources, you will see the message "Connection was made successfully." Click *OK* to close the message box.

The Data Source Name dialog box reappears.

6) Click *OK*, then click *Done* to close the Connections dialog box.

DEFINING A DATABASE CONNECTION FOR COLDFUSION

The database connection acts as the pipeline that connects your UltraDev pages to your database. In effect, it acts as a pointer for communication between the two and you'll only have to define one connection for most sites.

1) Open the Andes Tutorial site and choose Modify > Connections.

The Connections dialog box appears.

2) Click *New*, then select the ordinary DSN rather than the Advanced.

Provide a login ID and password for the *ColdFusion Remote Development Services (RDS)* if you are asked to do so.

Otherwise, the remainder of the procedure is the same as creating an ASP DSN.

ADDING A RECORDSET TO A PAGE

After you've made your data connection, you're almost ready to start putting data values on a page—but not quite.

For actual use on a page-by-page basis, you need a representation of just those parts of the data that are relevant to the task at hand. An entire database will often be too much to handle conveniently. Instead, it's much easier to use a subset of the data by creating a data query. The object you create for actual use on the page is known as a recordset in ASP and ColdFusion and as a resultset in JSP. The recordset or resultset is based on your data query. By the way, the recordset/resultset is tied to a specific page, not the entire site, so always make sure you have the desired page open—in this case product_detail—when you create a recordset.

1) Click either the Launcher's Data Bindings or Server Behaviors icon to open their respective panels.

You also can choose Window > Data Bindings or Window > Server Behaviors. It doesn't matter which panel you use, the destination is the same: the advanced Recordset dialog box.

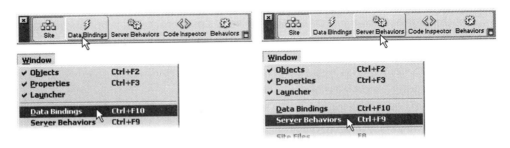

2) Click the + button in the Data Bindings or Server Behaviors panel and choose *Recordset (Query)* from the drop-down menu.

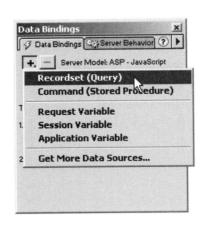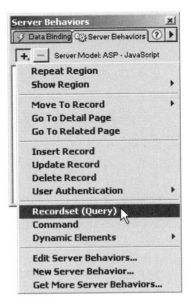

The simple Recordset dialog box that appears works well when you are building basic data queries that use just one data table. However, you're going to need data from two tables, so you'll want to open the advanced Recordset dialog box instead. (Sometimes the advanced Recordset dialog box may appear by default. The version of the dialog box last used—simple or advanced—dictates which one appears. It is initially confusing figuring out which version of the dialog box you are in. Just remember this: If you see a *Simple* button in the dialog box, then you're in the advanced version; if you see an *Advanced* button, you're in the simple version. If it helps, think of the button as an exit sign directing you to the other version.)

3) Click *Advanced* to open the advanced Recordset dialog box.

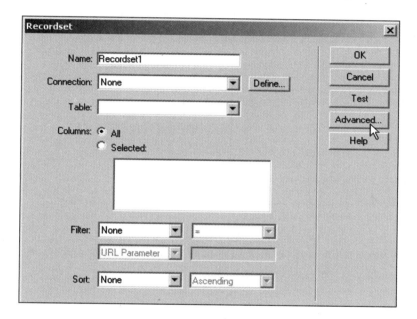

4) Type rsProducts **in the *Name* text field.**

Recordset names may not have spaces.

5) Select the data connection *connAndes* from the *Connection* drop-down menu (*connAndes* is probably your only choice at this point).

The database's *Tables*, *Views*, and *Stored Procedures* folders appear in the *Database Items* window.

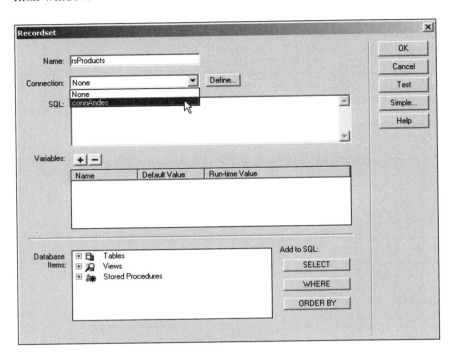

6) In the *Database Items* window click the + to expand the *Tables* folder and scroll through the folder until you find the *Products* table.

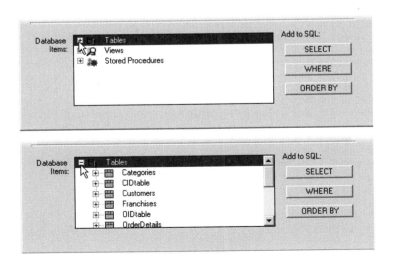

7) Highlight the *Products* data table and under *Add to SQL*, click SELECT.

In the *SQL* window, the SQL statement SELECT * FROM Products appears. The *
means "all fields," so every field within the *Products* table will be queried.

8) Click *Test*.

The entire *Products* data table appears in the Test SQL Statement pop-up window—
just as you'd expect from using the *. But the Products data table includes just an ID
number for each product's supplier. Suppose you need to know details about the
supplier of each product. Because many products share the same supplier, repeating
the supplier's name, address, phone number, and so on for every product would be
inefficient. Instead, you can use SQL to create a cross-reference between a product's
SupplierID field and the Suppliers data table, which contains details about each
supplier. That's covered in the next task—Adding a Cross-Referenced Recordset to a

Page—so click *OK* to close the Test SQL Statement pop-up window but leave the Recordset dialog box open. If you need to take a break, choose File > Save to preserve the rsProducts recordset before quitting UltraDev.

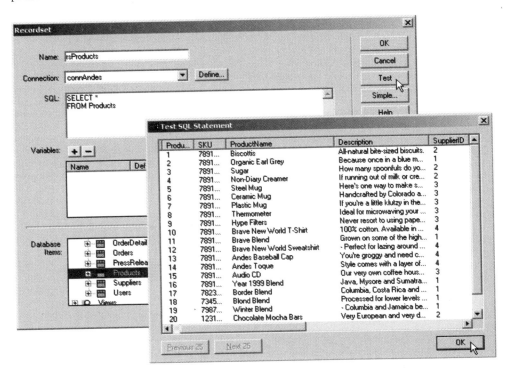

NOTE *Structured Query Language (SQL) serves as the common language of ODBC and JDBC databases. SQL (pronounced "sequel") is basically a notation language for extracting needed data from a relational database. While SQL can get complicated, UltraDev's point-and-click approach fortunately means that you can get by with very little under-the-hood knowledge of SQL.*

ADDING A CROSS-REFERENCED RECORDSET TO A PAGE

As explained in Adding a Recordset to a Page on page 33, sometimes creating a basic recordset doesn't offer the precision or efficiency that's needed. By creating a cross-referenced, or relational, recordset, you can side-step that problem entirely.

If you closed the Andes Tutorial site's product_detail page after the previous exercise, reopen it and double-click *Recordset(rsProducts)* in the Server Behaviors palette to reach the Recordset dialog box.

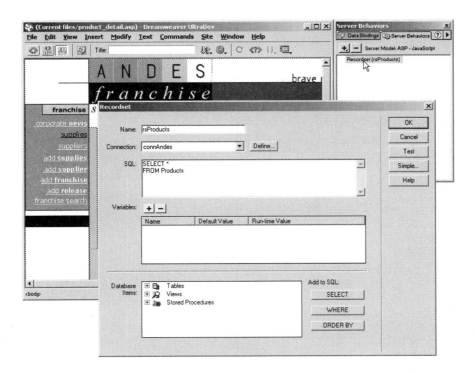

1) Expand the *Tables* folder in the Database Items window, highlight the *Suppliers* data table inside the folder, and click *SELECT* under *Add to SQL*.

The SQL statement, which had been SELECT * FROM Products changes to SELECT * FROM Products, Suppliers. (Whether you have a line break after the * makes no difference in the SQL statement.)

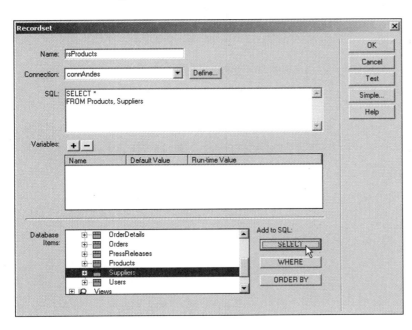

2) Expand the *Suppliers* data table, highlight the *SupplierID* field, and click *WHERE* under *Add to SQL*.

The WHERE clause, as it's called, filters the data returned by the SQL statement. The WHERE clause now reads WHERE SupplierID.

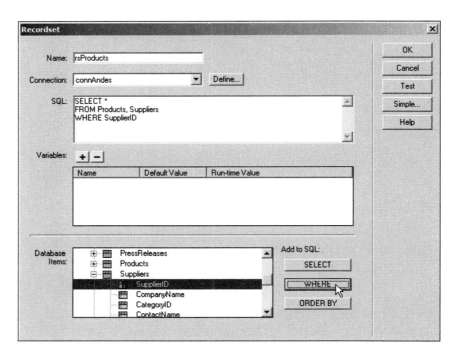

You need to edit the WHERE clause manually so that only records in which the SupplierID field is the same as in the Product and Suppliers tables are returned. You'll do so in the next step.

3) Type directly inside the *SQL* window to change WHERE Products.Supplier **to** WHERE Products.SupplierID = Suppliers.SupplierID.

Products is the first table name and the period separates it from SupplierID (the field name). The = sign joins this statement to Suppliers, which is the second table name, separated by a period from the matching field name, SupplierID.

(Whether you have spaces before and after the = makes no difference in the SQL statement. Be sure, however, that you type Suppliers and not Supplier.)

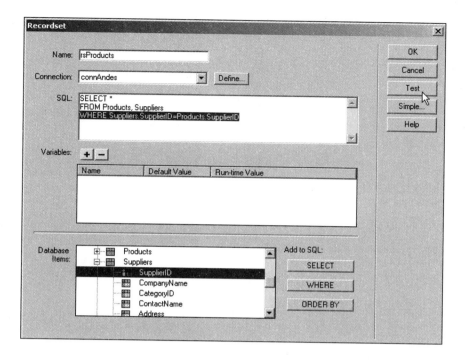

4) Click *Test* to test the SQL again.

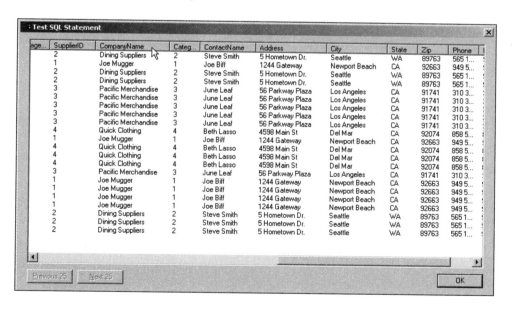

You see all the details of the supplier added to each record. Now suppose you want to filter the results to see only products sold by suppliers in California.

5) Highlight the *State* field in the *Suppliers* data table. Under *Add to SQL*, click *WHERE*.

The words AND State are added to the WHERE clause.

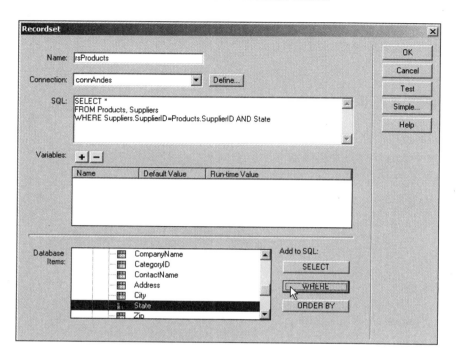

6) Type directly inside the *SQL* window to add ='CA' to edit the WHERE clause. The clause should now read: WHERE Suppliers.SupplierID = Products.SupplierID AND State ='CA'.

The reason you don't need to include Suppliers.State as part of AND State ='CA' is because there is no field named State in the Products table. Be sure to use single quote marks around the field value CA.

42

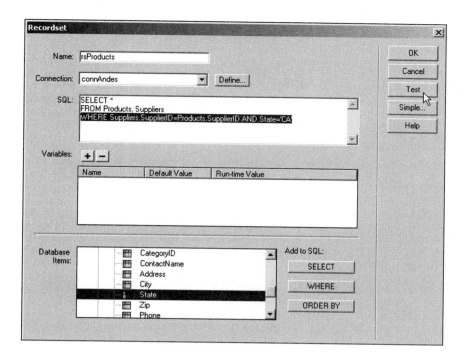

7) Click *Test* to test the SQL again.

Now you see only California-supplied products.

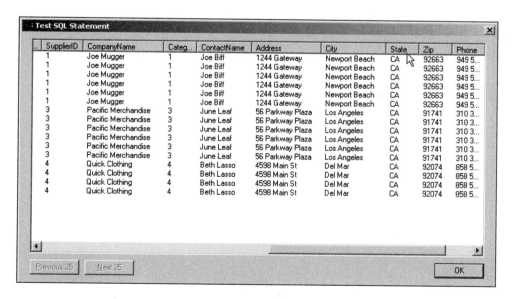

8) Delete AND State ='CA' **from the *SQL* window and click *OK* to close the dialog box.**

You don't need to filter for California suppliers in the next lesson, so you get rid of that part of the SQL statement.

9) Choose File > Save to preserve your SQL statement. Open the Data Bindings palette and double-click *Recordset (rsProducts)*.

The expanded recordset shows all the data fields that will be available for use in adding dynamic data to the product_detail page in the next lesson.

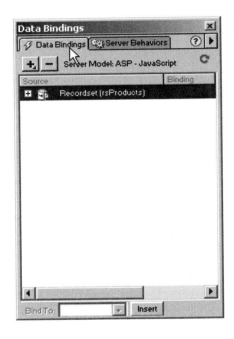
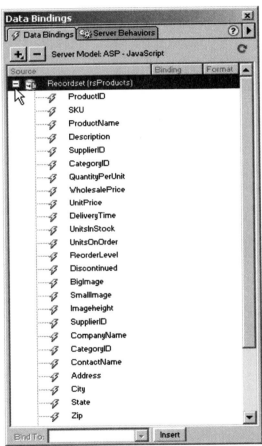

WHAT YOU HAVE LEARNED

In this lesson, you have:

- Configured your database connection to work with the specific server model you're using: ASP, JSP, or ColdFusion (pages 30–33)

- Created a simple recordset (or a resultset in JSP) for your site's product detail page, using a Structured Query Language statement (pages 33–38)

- Used SQL to refine the recordset's precision by adding cross-references between the database's products and suppliers tables (pages 38–44)

adding dynamic data

LESSON 4

Starting with this lesson, you'll begin to create pages that use live data components. These components form an essential part of UltraDev's ability to link Web pages with database records and fields. This lesson runs a bit longer than some others, but it provides the foundation for many of the tasks in later lessons. Before starting, take a look at the figure below to understand the overall logic and connection among the Andes Coffee Web site's main pages:

The **Search** page lets users find product information by applying one or more search criteria. You will build this page in Lesson 8.

The **Results** page displays in abbreviated form the products that meet the search criteria. In each listing, the product name is a hyperlink, enabling the user to click it to open a page with all the details of a product. You will build this page in Lesson 5.

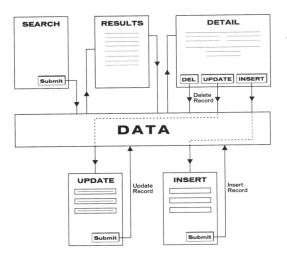

The information flow among the main pages of the Andes Coffee Web site. You will add dynamic functions to these pages in Lessons 4–8.

The **Detail** page acts as a basic catalog page. You created a recordset for this page in Lesson 3; you'll complete the page in this lesson. Eventually it will include navigation buttons so that users can browse the sorted catalog. It also will include Insert, Update, and Delete buttons.

The **Update** page lets site administrators edit product data records via an online form. You will build this page in Lesson 7.

The **Insert** page lets site administrators create a completely new product data record, using an online form. It looks similar to the Update page, but its fields are initially blank, whereas the Update page's fields contain data for editing. You will build the Insert page in Lesson 6.

WHAT YOU WILL LEARN

In this lesson, you will:

- Dynamically link Web page text and images to a database
- Add Live Objects to your pages
- Use the Live Data View to see data placed in Web pages
- Bind a variety of Form Objects to database records

APPROXIMATE TIME

This lesson takes approximately 90 minutes to complete.

LESSON FILES

Media Files:

Various image files within UltraDev 4 Lessons\ASP\Current files

Beginning Files:

UltraDev 4 Lessons\...\Current files\product_detail

UltraDev 4 Lessons\...\Current files\product_update

Completed Files:

Same as Beginning Files, plus Current files\heightbind_demo

MAKING TEXT DYNAMIC

In Lesson 3, you defined a database connection and used it to add a recordset to the product_detail page. Now you're all set to design the page using values from the Andes Coffee database (andescoffee.mdb).

1) Open the product_detail page if you closed it at the end of Lesson 3.

Notice that the page contains a table with seven types of preset information (starting with *SKU*), plus a more prominent field for the product name immediately above the picture. Under each of the seven data labels is an empty table cell. You're going to fill those cells with dynamic text pulled from the recordset created in Lesson 3.

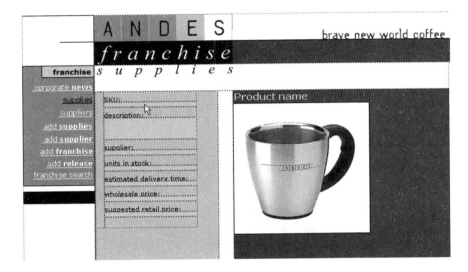

2) Place the cursor in the table cell just below the label *SKU*. With the Data Bindings panel open and displaying the expanded *rsProducts* recordset, select the field *SKU* and click the *Insert* button at the bottom right of the palette.

The design-time placeholder token *{rsProducts.SKU}* appears in the table cell. When viewed in a Web browser, this token will be replaced with the field's actual value for the selected record.

You also have the option of dragging the data source from the Data Bindings panel and dropping it into the table cell.

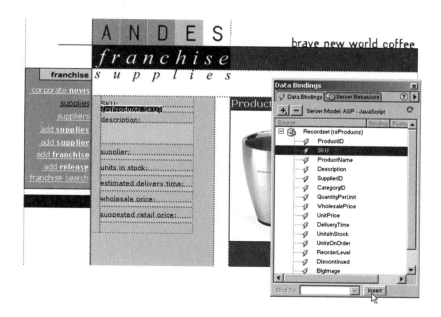

3) Repeat step 2 for the fields *description*, *supplier* (*CompanyName* in the recordset), *units in stock*, and *estimated delivery time*.

You'll need to insert the word *days* after *{rsProducts.DeliveryTime}*—the placeholder in the *estimated delivery time* field.

For these first five data fields, no special formatting is required. However, the remaining two—*wholesale price* and *suggested retail price*—need to be formatted as dollar amounts, using a $#,###.## format.

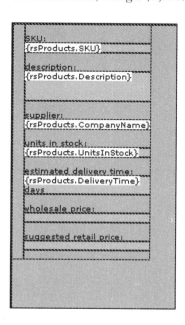

4) Insert the dynamic *WholesalePrice* in the page's *wholesale price* field, then click the down arrow in the *Format* column of the Data Bindings panel and select Currency > 2 Decimal Places.

The placeholder does not change its appearance but the $#,###.## format will be applied when you switch to the Live Data View or look at the page with your Web browser.

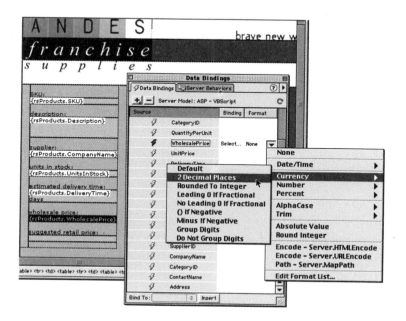

5) Insert the dynamic *UnitPrice* in the page's *suggested retail price* field, and again use the *Format* column's down arrow to select Currency > 2 Decimal Places.

The *suggested retail price* field will be tied to the database and appear with the proper $#,###.## format within the Live Data and browser views.

Now you need to replace the *Product name* that appears just above the product image with a dynamic product name.

6) Use your cursor to select the *Product name* placeholder text and delete it, then leave the cursor where it is. Select the *ProductName* field back in the Data Bindings panel and click *Insert*.

The placeholder *{rsProducts.ProductName}* will appear above the product image.

7) Save the page and click the Live Data View button to see what you've done so far.

The screen switches to a browser-like view and the placeholders are replaced with actual data from the rsProducts recordset. As you can see, however, that steel mug is no biscotti. The next task, adding dynamic images to the page, will fix that.

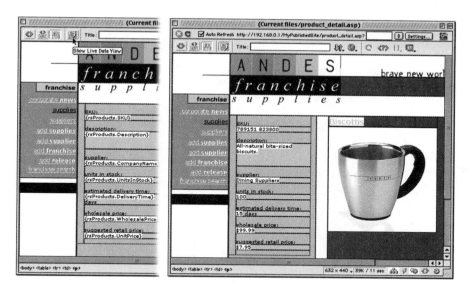

MAKING IMAGES DYNAMIC

Though the behind-the-scenes coding works a bit differently, adding dynamic images to a page works very similarly to creating dynamic text.

1) Make sure the product_detail page and the Data Bindings panel are open, and click on the page's large image to select it.

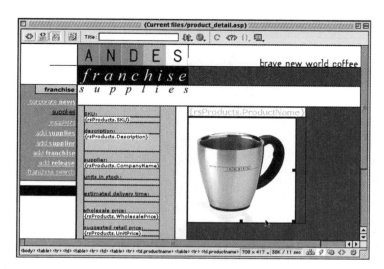

2) Select the *BigImage* data field in the Data Bindings panel and click the *Insert* button at the bottom of the palette.

The placeholder image will be replaced with a generic image icon.

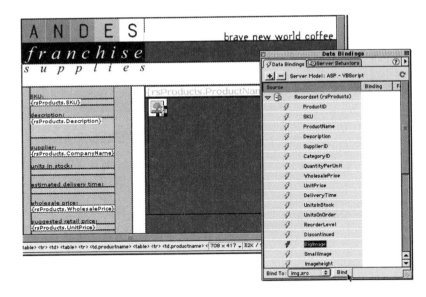

3) Save the page and click the Live Data View button.

Once UltraDev switches to the Live Data View, the generic image icon is replaced with a product image that reflects the product name and product description.

You still have no way of moving from product to product, so the next task will be to add a navigation bar, using UltraDev's Server-Behavior-based Live Objects.

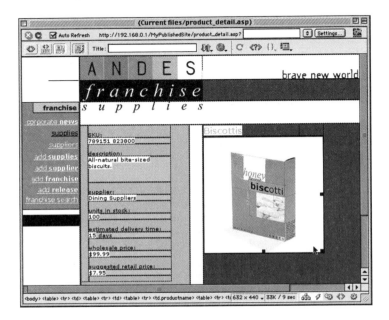

Adding dynamic images to a page involves binding a placeholder image to a field in the recordset. By default, UltraDev uses the img src *tag. If you click the* bigimage *field's Binding drop-down menu, however, you can bind to any of 21 image attributes—including its height or width, which can be handy if the size of the images varies greatly. For a detailed example of this ability, see Binding Other HTML Attributes on page 78.*

ADDING A LIVE OBJECT

Using a navigation bar to browse from page to page is nothing new. But UltraDev gives navigation bars new powers thanks to Live Objects, which use application server behaviors that interact with your data recordset.

1) Place the cursor at the bottom of the product detail page, just above the copyright line.

This is where you'll be inserting the navigation bar, though in general you're free to place navigation objects like this anywhere you have room on a page.

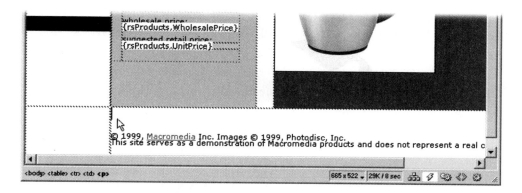

2) Make sure the Objects palette is visible (Ctrl+F2 Windows or Command+F2 Mac) and select *Live* from the drop-down menu.

The Objects panel will switch to show UltraDev's Live Objects.

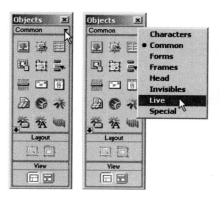

53

3) Click the Insert Recordset Navigation Bar icon in the Live Objects panel, choose the *Images* radio button in the dialog box that appears, and click *OK*.

A set of four arrows with *Show If…* labels appears where you first clicked your cursor in step 1. If you choose *Text*, HTML text (*First*, *Previous*, *Next*, and *Last*) will be inserted instead of arrow images.

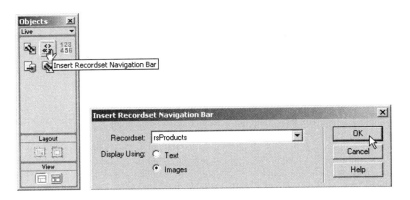

4) Click the far-left arrow's *Show If…* label, then open the Server Behaviors panel.

In the panel, you'll see that the dynamic behavior has been attached to the image. The *Show If Not First Record* behavior will suppress display of the arrow if the Live Data View or browser preview is displaying the rsProduct recordset's very first record since there wouldn't be a previous record to move to. The navigation bar's other three arrows also have dynamic server behaviors attached to them. The power of this and other Live Objects will be explained more fully in upcoming lessons.

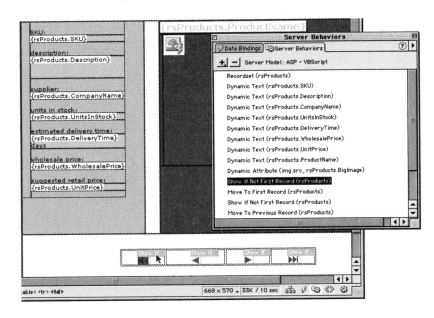

5) Switch to the Site panel's *Local Folder* and select the four arrow image files (*First.gif, Previous.gif, Next.gif*, and *Last.gif*). Use the Put button to transfer them to the server's *Remote Site*.

The four image files will be transferred to the Remote Site and appear in the left-hand pane of the Site panel.

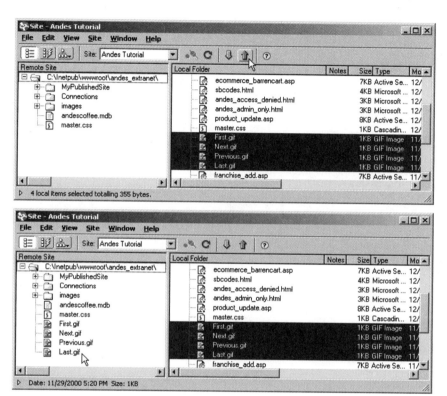

6) Switch back to the product detail page, save it and click the File Management button to transfer it to the Remote Site as well.

55

7) Press F12 (or click the Preview in Browser button).

Using data and images pulled from the rsProducts recordset, your Web browser will display the first record in the product detail page. As noted in step 4, the first record does not display the First and Previous arrows. Click to the second record, however, and all four arrows will appear—reflecting the server behaviors attached the Live Object navigation bar.

With the navigation bar in place, you can use your Web browser to move through all the records. UltraDev also offers a second way to see your pages with live data—the Live Data view—which you'll learn to use in the next task.

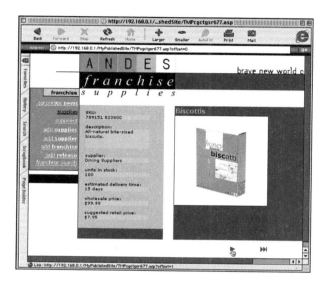

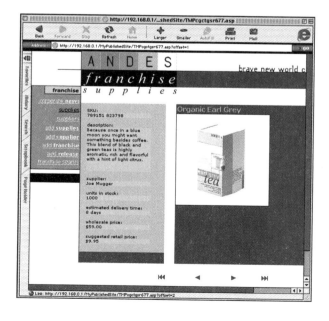

USING THE LIVE DATA VIEW

Unlike browser preview, UltraDev's Live Data View displays your page with dynamic data pulled from the recordset and lets you adjust the layout of your pages on the fly. The Live Data View also lets you use queries to move through records. Instead of constantly toggling between UltraDev's Design View and your Web browser, you can see it all within Live Data View.

1) Switch to Live Data View by clicking its button in the toolbar or choosing View > Live Data (Ctrl+Shift+R Windows or Command+Shift+R Mac).

The product detail page will display data from the first record in the recordset. Notice that the top of the window now displays the page's URL on the Remote Server, along with a gear icon in the upper right denoting that the Live Data View is active.

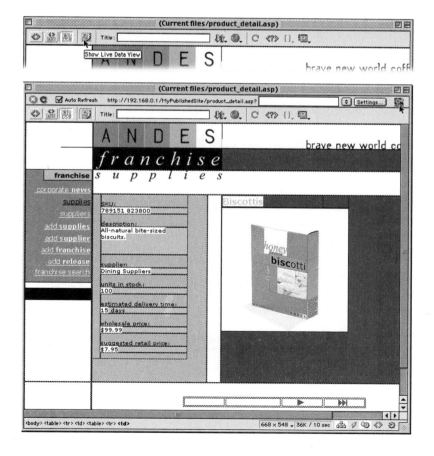

2) Type index=3 **into the query string window (just right of the URL) and click the refresh button (Ctrl+R Windows or Command+R Mac).**

The Live Data View will now display the fourth record in the set (index=0 would be the first record). By changing the query string number, you can jump directly to any record.

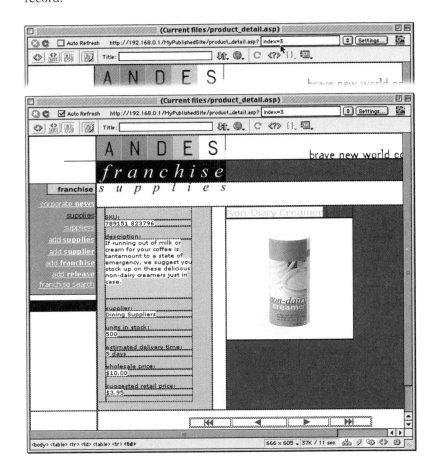

TIP *If you check the* Auto Refresh *box, you can then just press Enter (Windows) or Return (Macintosh) after typing in a new query string and the new record will be displayed automatically.*

3) Click the *Settings* button, check the *Save Settings For This Document* box in the Live Data Settings dialog box, and click *OK*.

The index value will be saved in the Live Data View's query string window—enabling you to jump directly to a particular record whenever you switch to Live Data View.

58

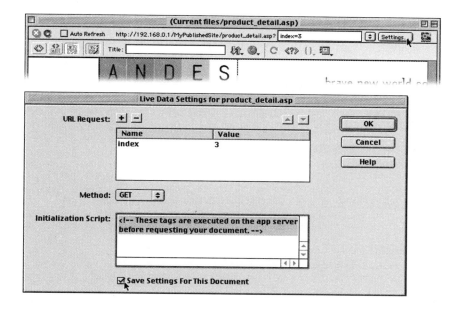

TIP *You change the index value by typing a new number into the query string window or in the Live Data Settings dialog box's* Value *column.*

4) Click the Live Data View button again when you want to switch back to UltraDev's Design View. Save and close the product_detail page.

NOTE *The Live Data View cannot move dependent files from the Local Folder to the Remote Site—even if you click* Yes *in the Dependent Files dialog box. For that reason, any local files created while in Live Data View must be manually moved to the Remote Folder by selecting them in the Local Folder and then using the Put button.*

MAKING FORM OBJECTS DYNAMIC

Just like images, form objects can be dynamically linked to a recordset by binding their values to specific recordset fields. This was the method used in Making Images Dynamic on page 51. As you'll see in the remainder of this lesson, text fields, menus, check boxes, and radio buttons can be bound in this way.

A typical use for this type of linking would be to bring a complete record into a whole suite of form text fields to create an update page. That makes the existing data available for editing, and the action of submitting the form updates the record itself to conform to the edited page. You'll use this type of linking extensively in Lesson 7, but you will get a feel for the procedure in the rest of this lesson by creating a new recordset and then binding various form objects to that data.

1) Open the product_update page. Click the + button in either the Data Bindings or Server Behaviors panel and choose *Recordset(Query)* from the drop-down menu.

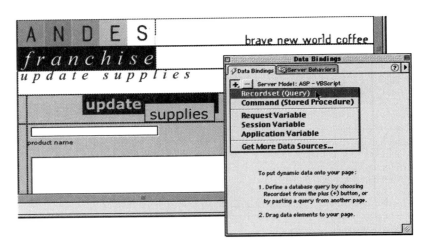

2) Type rsUpdate **in the *Name* field of the Recordset dialog box.**

If the dialog box opens with advanced form displayed, switch to the simple form by clicking the *Simple* button. (If the *Advanced* button appears, you're already in the simple form.)

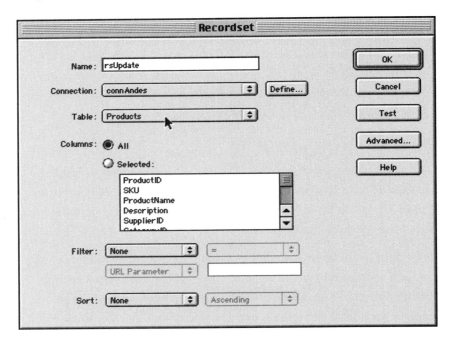

3) Use the pop-up menus to select the *connAndes* connection and the *Products* data table.

By using a radio button and a list selector, you could exclude some data columns from the recordset. However, in this case you want to leave *All* columns selected.

4) Click *Test* to make sure that the data is being returned correctly and, if it is, click *OK* to close the Test SQL Statement dialog box.

The reason a new recordset is required here is that this page will ultimately write edited data into the database instead of just reading existing database entries. Data reads can come from any number of joined tables, but data writes can be done only to a single table.

5) Click *OK* to close the Recordset dialog box.

The Data Bindings panel will show all the recordset fields tied to the product update page. Now you're ready to bind the fields to various form objects.

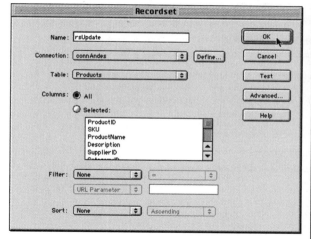

61

ADDING DYNAMIC DATA

BINDING FORM TEXT FIELDS TO DATA

Binding form text fields to data is the simplest, but often the most used, of the various form objects.

1) Open the product_update page, click the ⟨*form*⟩ tag in the document's tag selector, and when the Property Inspector panel opens, type AndesUpdate **in the** *Form Name* **text field.**

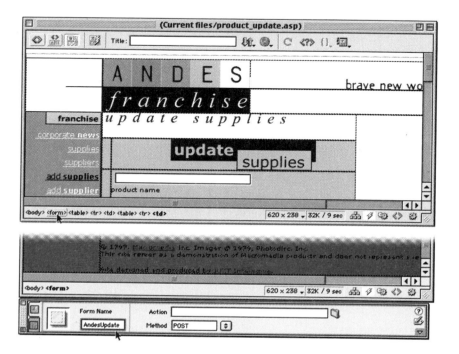

While you don't have to name the form, doing so makes it possible to control it later on with VBScript, JavaScript, or another scripting language, so it's a good habit to form.

2) Click in the product_update page's *product name* **field to select it. Select** *ProductName* **in the Data Bindings panel and click the** *Bind* **button at the bottom of the panel.**

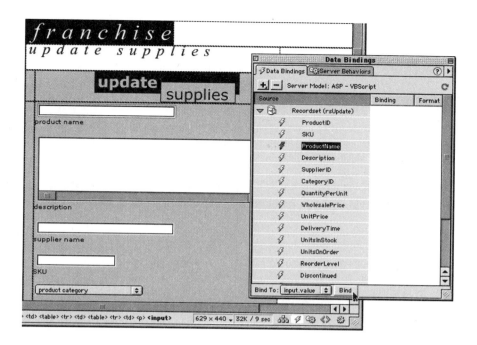

The *product name* field in the product_update page is now bound to the ProductName field in the rsUpdate recordset. UltraDev signals the binding in three places: the *{rsUpdate.ProductName}* placeholder appears in the *product name* field, *input.value* appears next to *ProductName* in the Data Bindings panel, and the Bind button now says *Unbind*.

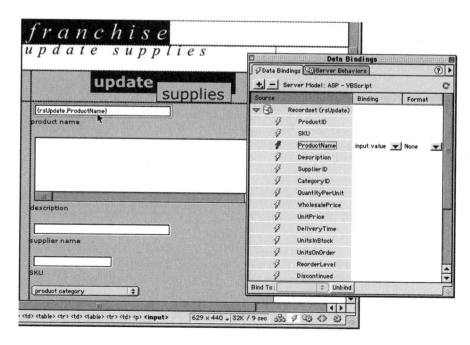

BINDING MENUS AND LISTS TO DATA

Often you will need to bind a menu or drop-down list to data in two ways. First you may need to populate the list from a data table. Then you may want to preset the selection so it corresponds to the value of some field in a record the page is displaying. That record may come from a different recordset. This update page offers a perfect example of this since the product category menu needs to be populated somehow and then preset from the rsUpdate recordset.

1) With the product_update page open, click the + button in either the Data Bindings or Server Behaviors panel, and choose *Recordset(Query)* from the drop-down menu.

To populate the menu, you will first need to create a new recordset, this time pulling data from the Categories data table.

2) Type rsCategories in the *Name* field of the Recordset dialog box.

The simple version of the Recordset dialog box should be visible, but if it's not just click the *Simple* button.

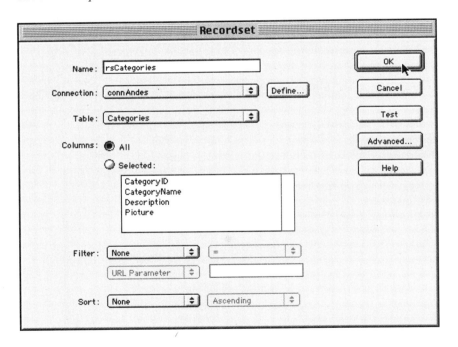

3) Use the *Connection* and *Table* pop-up menus to select the *connAndes* connection and the *Categories* data. Click *OK* to close the dialog box.

Leave the *Columns* button set to *All.*

4) Select the *product category* menu element on the product_update page, click the + button in the Server Behaviors panel and choose Dynamic Elements > Dynamic List/Menu.

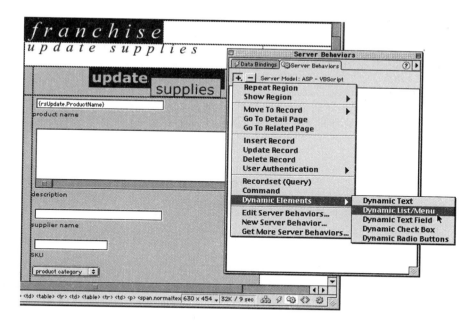

5) Make sure that *rsCategories* is selected in the *Recordset* pop-up menu.

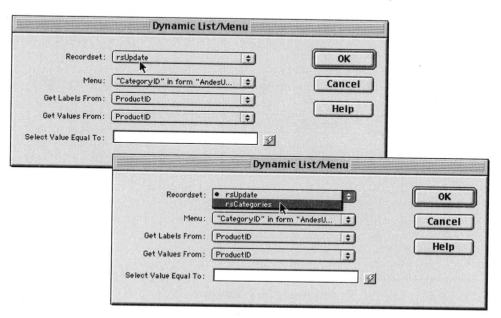

Take a close look since the *rsUpdate* recordset may appear initially instead.

6) Use the *Get Labels From* pop-up menu to select *CategoryName*.

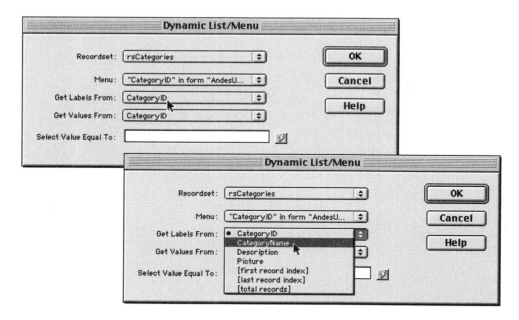

Initially the *Get Labels From* menu displays the *CategoryID* field, which pulls product ID numbers from the database. That's fine for computers but it will be nicer for the people updating the page's records if the pop-up menu displays recognizable names of merchandise categories—which is exactly what the *CategoryName* field contains. This ability to display one thing (labels) for users and pull numbers (values) from elsewhere in the database is just one of the powerful features built into UltraDev.

7) Click the lightning-bolt icon to the right of the *Select Value Equal To* text field.

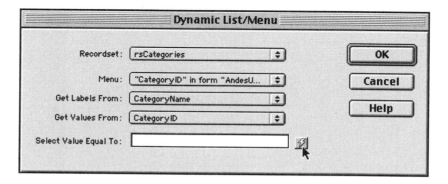

The Dynamic Data dialog box will open.

8) Click the arrow next to *Recordset(rsUpdate)*, select the *CategoryID* field when the recordset expands, and click *OK* to close the Dynamic Data dialog box.

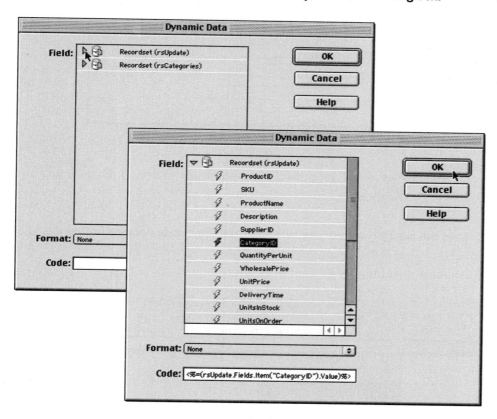

This enables you to switch from the rsCategories recordset to the rsUpdate recordset, which contains the CategoryID values you want to use. When the Dynamic List/Menu dialog box reappears, the code inside the *Select Value Equal To* window (`<%=(rsUpdate.Fields.Item("CategoryID").Value)%>`) indicates that the rsUpdate recordset will be the source for the CategoryID value.

9) Click _OK_ to close the Dynamic List/Menu dialog box.

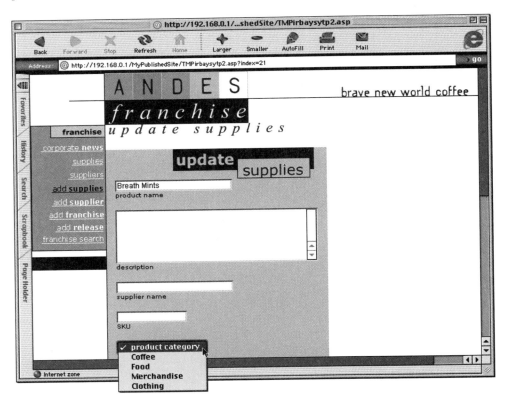

Once the dialog box closes, the Server Behaviors panel will display the dynamic list behavior you just created.

10) Save the product_update page and click the Preview in Browser button (F12).
Your Web browser will display the product_update page and, when clicked, the product _category_ menu will contain names, not numbers.

BINDING CHECK BOXES TO DATA

A check box works well for binding to a true-or-false (Boolean) data field. While the product_update page doesn't appear to contain any check boxes, in fact there's a Boolean field in the rsUpdate recordset for discontinued product lines. Using UltraDev's Dynamic Check Box dialog box, you can have a box automatically checked if that field is true in the database record.

1) Open the product_update page, click just above the *Update* button, and type `discontinued?` **(with the question mark).**

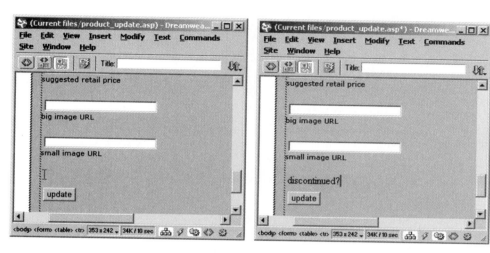

2) Select Forms from the Objects palette's drop-down menu, then click the Check Box icon.

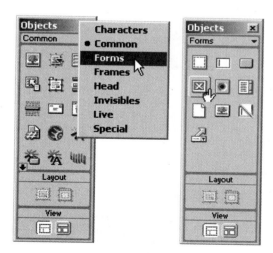

A check box will be added to the product_update page at the insertion point.

3) Open the Property Inspector (Ctrl+F3 Windows or Command+F3 Mac) and name the checkbox Discontinued.

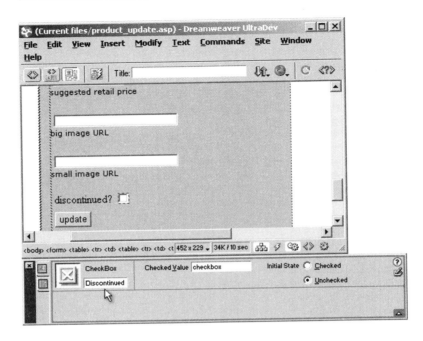

4) With the checkbox still selected on the product_update page, click the + button in the Server Behaviors panel and choose Dynamic Elements > Dynamic Check Box from the drop-down menu.

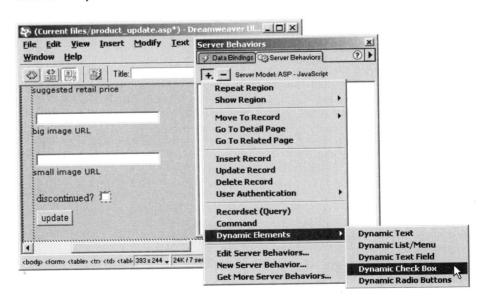

The Dynamic Check Box dialog box will appear.

5) Click the dialog box's lightning-bolt icon to the right of the *Check If* field.

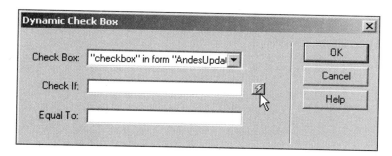

6) Click the + button to expand *Recordset(rsUpdate)* in the Dynamic Data dialog box, select the *Discontinued* field in the expanded list, and click *OK*.

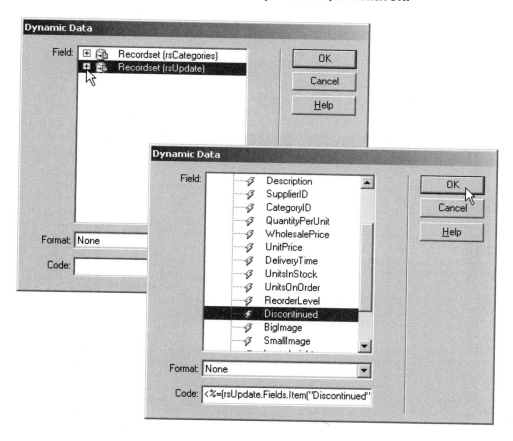

The Dynamic Check Box dialog box will reappear with the Discontinued field reference added to the *Check If* text window.

7) Type `true` **in the initially empty** *Equal To* **text window and click** *OK* **to close the dialog box. Save the page (Ctrl+S Windows, Command+S Mac).**

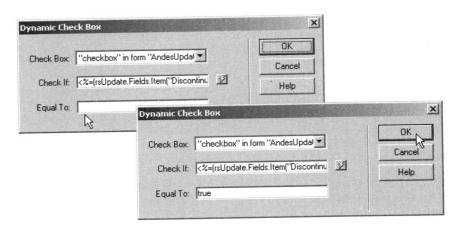

UltraDev now will fill in the *discontinued?* check box whenever the product_update page displays a product that has been labeled discontinued in the database. The Live Data View will let you see this new server behavior in action.

8) Click the product_update page's Live Data View button, type `index=21` **into the query window, and click the Refresh button to see the last record in Live Data View.**

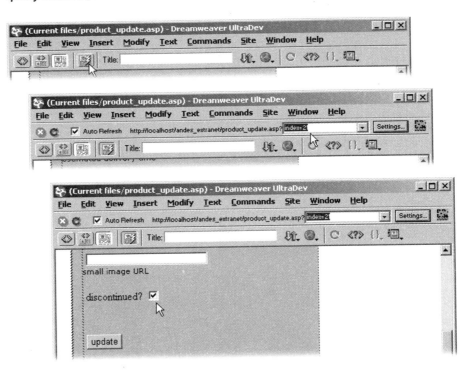

The last product in the database, index 21 (Breath mints), will be displayed in the Live Data View. This item was already marked as discontinued in the database and, as a result, if you scroll down the page, you'll see that the *discontinued?* box has been checked.

T I P *If you checked the Live Data View's* Auto Refresh *button ahead of time, you won't need to keep using the Refresh button to see your results.*

BINDING RADIO BUTTONS TO DATA

Radio buttons work well when the user of the page must choose from a limited number of possibilities. The rsUpdate recordset contains a data field— Estimated Delivery Time—that offers exactly this sort of limited range of choices. The value can be only 30, 15, 8, or 5 days, so you will add a set of four radio buttons as a way of allowing that choice.

1) Open the product_update page, select the existing *estimated delivery time* text field, and delete it.

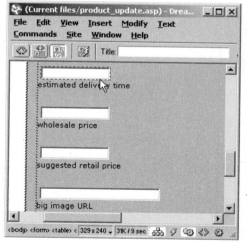 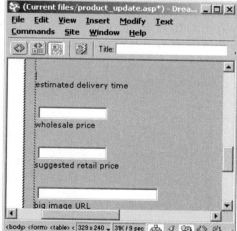

2) Use the Radio Button icon in the Objects palette to add four radio buttons located where the text field was.

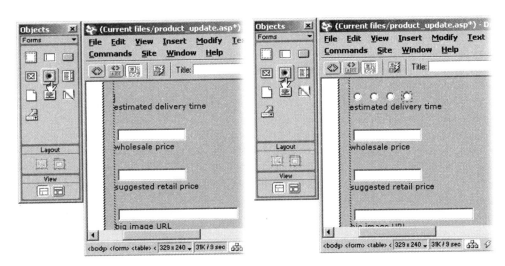

3) Type a label for each button (30, 15, 8, and 5 respectively) and add , days to the *estimated delivery time* field label.

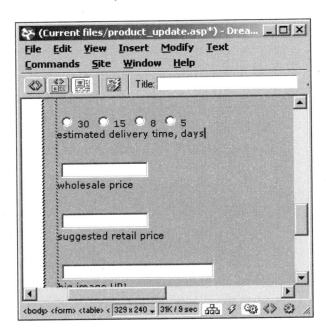

4) Click the first radio button to select it. Use the Property Inspector to name the first button Delivery Time **and type** 30 **into the Checked Value text window. Name the remaining three radio buttons** Delivery Time **as well, but give them checked values of** 15, 8, **and** 5 **respectively.**

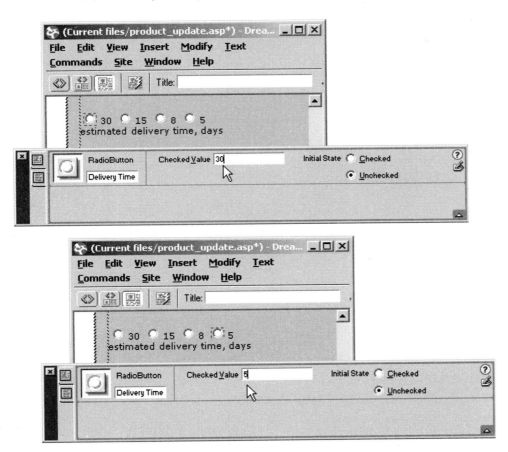

As you can see in the Property Inspector, all four buttons are not checked by default (based on the *Initial State*). The number in the *Checked Value* window determines the field's value once it is checked.

5) Select any of the four radio buttons, click the + button in the Server Behaviors panel and choose *Dynamic Elements > Dynamic Radio Buttons* from the drop-down menu.

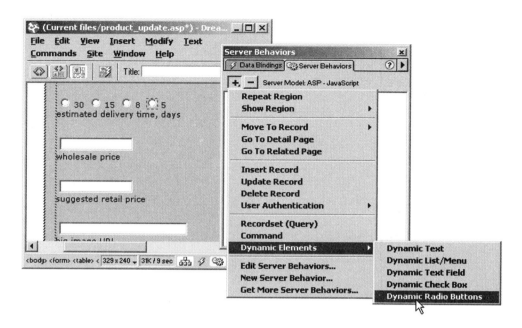

The Dynamic Radio Buttons dialog box will display four different values for the four identically named *Delivery Time* buttons. Check the numbers in the *Radio Button Values* text field to make sure you made no typos. Corrections can be made by selecting any number in the *Radio Button Values* text field and typing the correct number in the *Value* text field.

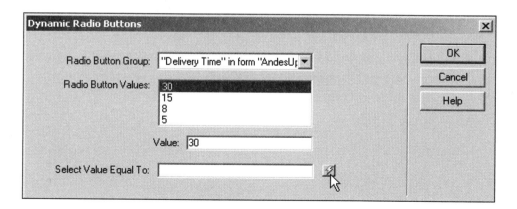

6) Click the lightning-bolt icon in the Dynamic Radio Buttons dialog box.

7) Click the arrow next to *Recordset(rsUpdate)*, select the *DeliveryTime* field from the expanded recordset, and click *OK* to close the Dynamic Data dialog box.

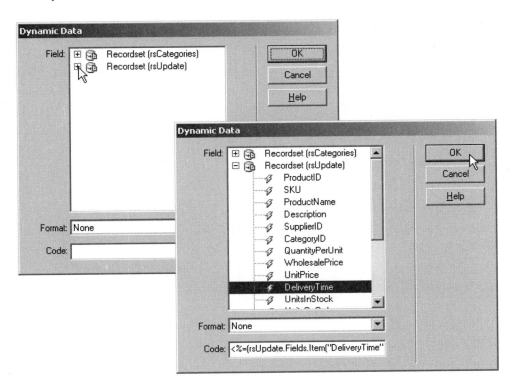

8) Click *OK* to close the Dynamic Radio Buttons dialog box when it reappears. Save the page (Ctrl+S Windows, Command+S Macintosh).

9) Click the product_update page's Live Data View button, where you'll find that *index=21* **remains in the query window. Click the Refresh button, scroll down to the** *estimated delivery time* **field, and you will see that the** *30* **radio button is activated.**

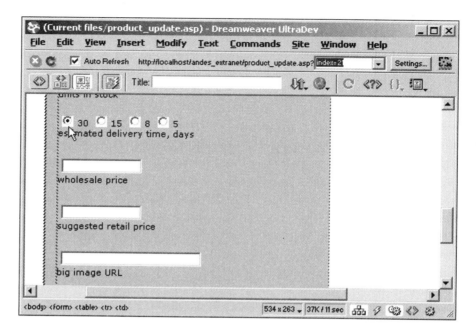

BINDING OTHER HTML ATTRIBUTES

You've already seen how the SRC attribute of an image can be made dynamic, and you may have considered that other HTML attributes such as WIDTH, HEIGHT, and ALT could also be made dynamic. In principle, any attribute of any HTML tag can be bound to a data field so that it reflects the current value of that field.

There's a general way of displaying attributes so that data sources may easily be invoked to supply dynamic values. You're going to use this approach to create a page that binds a couple of unusual image attributes to recordset fields, showing discontinued products in a much more dramatic way than a simple check box. While this task runs longer than most, the lessons it offers go to the heart of what makes UltraDev's dynamic data capabilities so powerful.

1) Create a new page by choosing File > New (Ctrl+N Windows, Command+N Mac) and type Product Picture Page **in the page's** *Title* **text field.**

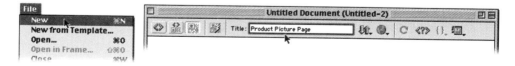

2) Name the page *heightbind_demo* and save it to your site.

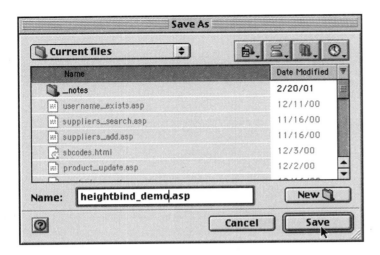

The proper file extension will be automatically added depending on whether you are working with the ASP, JSP, or ColdFusion server model.

3) Create a new recordset by clicking the + button in either the Data Bindings or Server Behaviors panel and choosing *Recordset(Query)* from the drop-down menu.

4) Name the new recordset rsProdpic, choose *connAndes* as the *Connection* and *Products* as the *Table*. Choose the *Selected* radio button and select these fields from the list: *ProductID*, *ProductName*, *Description*, *BigImage*, and *Imageheight*. Click *OK* to close the dialog box.

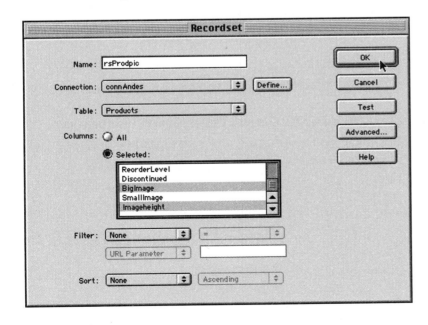

To select multiple, non-contiguous fields in the list, Ctrl+click (Windows) or Command+click (Mac).

5) Use the Common Objects panel's Layer icon, in combination with the Property Inspector, to draw a layer on the page at L(eft) *300*, T(op) *75*, W(idth) *225*, and H(eight) *225*.

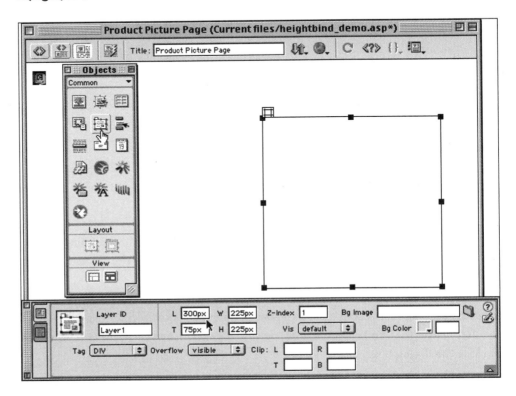

TIP *You can draw the layer freehand and then fill in the inspector's* L, T, W, *and* H *boxes to position and size the layer exactly.*

6) Click inside the layer, then click the Common Objects panel's Insert Image icon. When the Select Image Source dialog box opens, navigate to your site's *product_images* folder and open any of the *xx_Big.jpg* images.

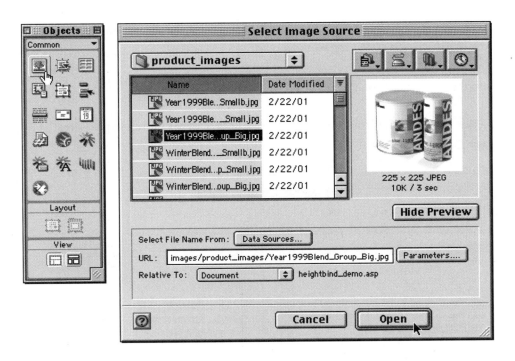

The image will be inserted into the new layer.

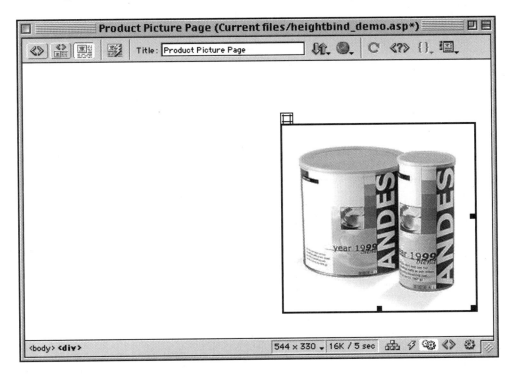

7) In the Property Inspector for the image, click the left-hand List tab and select *src* in the *Attributes for <IMG> tag* window.

If there is a lightning-bolt icon at the right side of the *src* attribute, click it, and skip to step 9. If you see a folder icon instead, go to step 8.

8) Click the *src* folder icon and then click the *Data Sources* button in the Select Image Source dialog box.

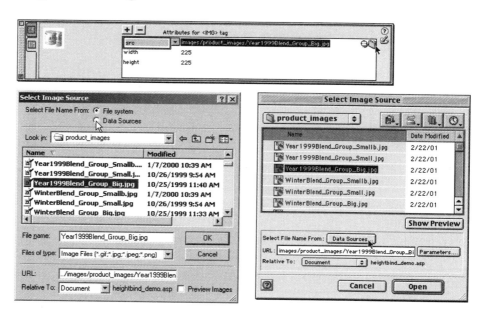

In Windows, the *Data Sources* radio button is near the top of the dialog box; on the Mac, a regular button sits toward the bottom.

9) Select the *BigImage* field in the Dynamic Data dialog box and click *OK*.

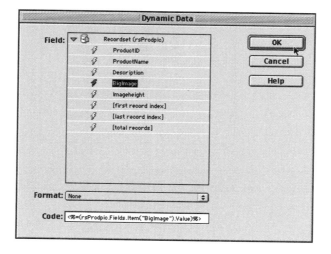

In the Property Inspector, the src image tag has been bound to the BigImage field in the rsProdpic recordset. In the layer, the original image has been replaced by a placeholder image that includes a lightning bolt: a sign that this image is now dynamic. This is just another way of binding an image to data, first explained in Making Images Dynamic on page 51.

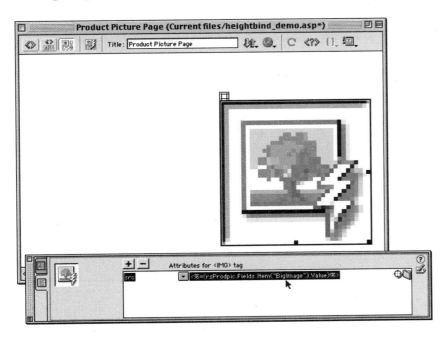

10) To bind another HTML attribute to the image, click the + button in the Property Inspector, then use the new blank field's drop-down menu to choose *alt*.

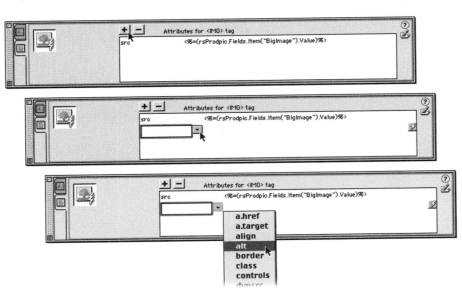

11) Click the *alt* tag's far-right lightning-bolt icon and select the *Description* field in the Dynamic Data dialog box. Click *OK* to close the dialog box.

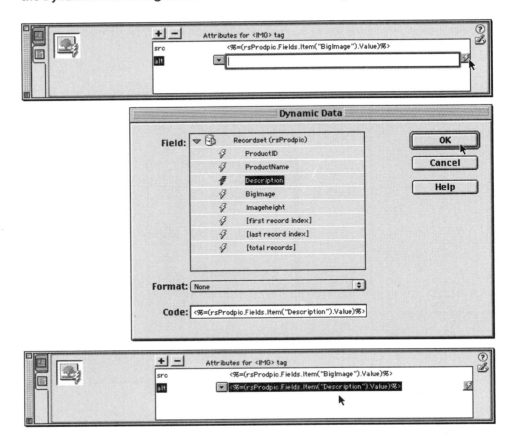

As you can see in the Property Inspector, the *alt* tag has been bound to the rsProdpic recordset's Description field.

12) Use the Common Objects panel's Layer icon, in combination with the Property Inspector, to draw a second layer at *L*(eft*) 300, T*(op*) 75, W*(idth*) 225,* and *H*(eight*) 45.*
This second layer will overlap the first layer, though it will be shorter.

13) With the layer still selected, click the Property Inspector's *Bg Color* drop-down menu and select the box with the red slash.

The red-slash box will make the layer's background color transparent, which means that the underlying product image (layer 1) will be visible if there's no image in layer 2.

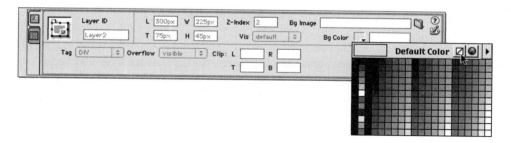

14) Click inside the new layer (layer 2), then click the Common Objects panel's Insert Image icon. When the Select Image Source dialog box opens, navigate to your site's *product_images* folder and open the *discont.gif* image.

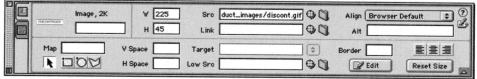

The Discontinued image will appear in the second layer, but UltraDev can make its appearance dynamic, based on whether a product really has been discontinued, by linking the image back to the database.

15) Click the List tab for the Property Inspector, click the far-right lightning-bolt icon for the *height* tag, and select the *Imageheight* field in the Dynamic Data dialog box. Click *OK* to close the dialog box.

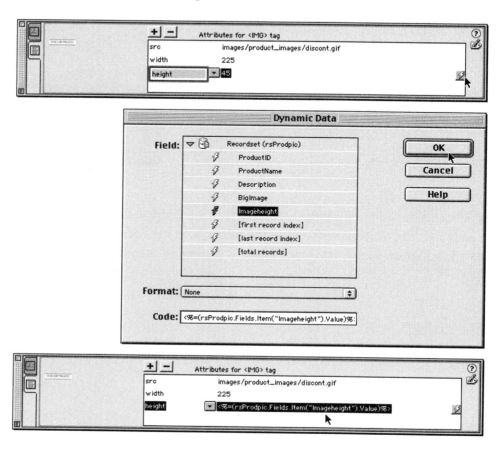

As you can see in the Property Inspector, the *height* tag has been bound to the rsProdpic recordset's Imageheight field. For most products, the height is 1 pixel, so the image will just look like a decorative red line (HTML does not allow the IMG HEIGHT attribute to be zero). But discontinued products have the number 45 in the Imageheight field. The effect will be that the 45-pixels-deep discontinued.gif will appear on top of the product's main image.

16) Choose Windows > CSS Styles (Ctrl+F11 Windows, Command+F11 Macintosh) to open the CSS Styles panel, click the Attach Style Sheet button at the bottom of the palette, and navigate to open the *master.css* file in your site.

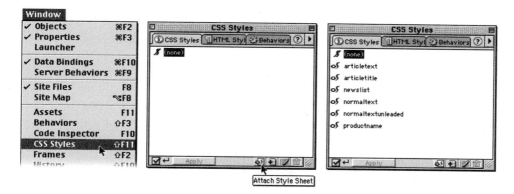

The styles contained in the master.css file will be added to the Styles panel—making them available for you to apply to the next layer you'll create.

17) Use the Common Objects panel's Layer icon, in combination with the Property Inspector, to draw a third layer at *L*(eft) *35*, *T*(op) *58*, *W*(idth) *265*, and *H*(eight) *34*.

18) Click inside the new layer, select *ProductName* in the Data Bindings panel, and click the panel's *Insert* button to bind the layer text to the field.

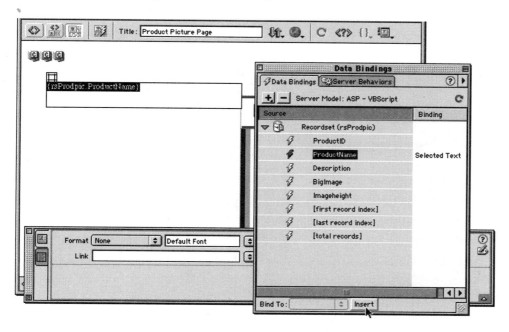

The placeholder text *{rsProdpic.ProductName}* will be pasted into the layer—binding it to the recordset's *ProductName* field.

19) With the cursor still inside the new layer, click *productname* in the CSS Styles panel.

The placeholder text will change to match the *productname* CSS style.

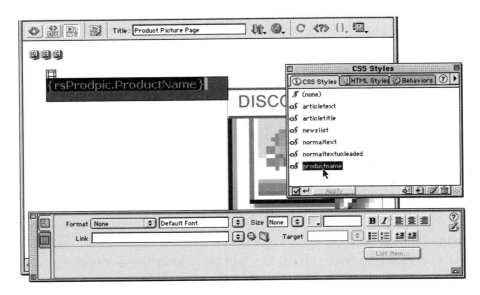

20) Select the layer itself, then click the *Bg Color* drop-down menu in the Property Inspector, and choose black (*#000000*).

The layer's background color will be changed to black.

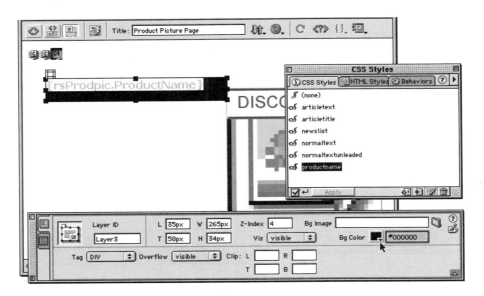

21) Use the Common Objects panel's Layer icon, in combination with the Property Inspector, to draw a fourth, final layer at L(eft) *35,* T(op) *125.*

22) Click inside the new layer, then click the Insert Recordset Navigation Bar icon in the Live Objects panel and choose the *Images* radio button. Click *OK* to close the dialog box.

A set of four navigation arrows will appear in the new layer.

23) Save the page, click the page's File Management button, and choose Put (Ctrl+Shift+U Windows, Command+Shift+U Mac) to move the file to the Remote Server. Click *Yes* when asked if you want to include dependent files.

Finally, you're ready to see the results of all your work.

24) Click the Preview in Browser button (F12).

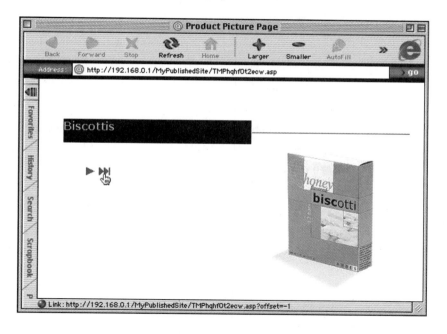

A picture of the first product in the recordset appears in your browser—complete with styled text, navigation arrows, and thin line above the picture. As you recall, the last product in the database, the breath mints has been discontinued, so let's take a look at it.

25) Click the last-record arrow in the browser.

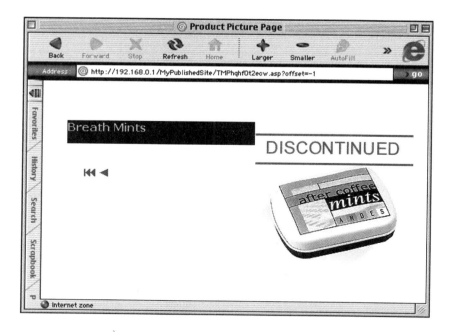

The discontinued image appears across the top of the product image. Anyone browsing this catalog will have no doubts about which products have been dropped. UltraDev's ability to dynamically link images and database information offers a great tool for creating dramatic, easy to understand Web pages.

WHAT YOU HAVE LEARNED

In this lesson, you have:

- Linked placeholder text to specific database fields, creating Web page text that changes based on the recordset queried (pages 48–51)

- Linked placeholder images to specific database fields, allowing product images to be dynamically served to a Web page (pages 51–53)

- Added a navigation bar that dynamically changes based on which product is being displayed (pages 53–57)

- Used the Live Data View to place dynamic data on a page, making it possible to accurately adjust a page's layout on the fly (pages 57–59)

- Added various Form Objects to a page and then bound the objects to specific recordset fields, making it possible to generate pages with dynamic text fields, menus, lists, checkboxes, or radio buttons (pages 59–78)

- Learned to bind virtually any HTML attribute to recordsets to generate visually dynamic Web pages (pages 78–90)

building multirecord result pages

In Lesson 4, you built a dynamic page that displays complete information for any one product. Using Live Data View, you saw how a change to the query string following the page's URL switched you from product to product, each representing a different record in the database.

Browsing record by record through a catalog database is certainly one way of making product information available to users, but it has obvious limitations if you have several hundred products. Much more often, e-commerce Web sites provide some means of searching the database, filtering for products that satisfy the user's search

In this lesson, you'll learn how to create a Web page like this one where every product listing is linked to a detailed product page.

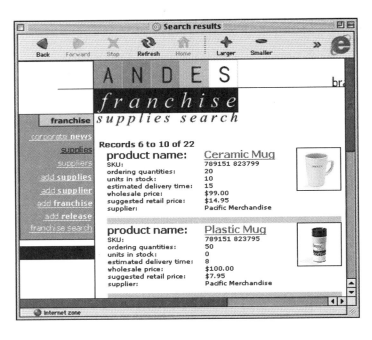

criteria, and then displaying a result list that provides brief details of each selected product. Every item on the result list includes a hyperlink to a detail page, which is the single-product page you already built. In this lesson, you will build a result list page, but without any search criteria. You'll build the search page in Lesson 8.

WHAT YOU WILL LEARN

In this lesson, you will:

- Copy a recordset from one page to another
- Repeat dynamic regions of a page
- Create your own live navigation bar for a page
- Add a navigation status display to a page
- Link a results page to a product details page

APPROXIMATE TIME

This lesson takes approximately 45 minutes to complete.

LESSON FILES

Media Files:

frm-first.gif, frm-previous.gif, frm-next.gif, and frm-last.gif (all in \Current files\images\)

Starting Files:

UltraDev 4 Lessons\...\Current files\product_detail

UltraDev 4 Lessons\...\Current files\product_resultlist

Completed Files:

Same as Beginning Files

COPYING A RECORDSET FROM PAGE TO PAGE

The skeleton of the result list page is available as product_resultlist, but it does not include a recordset. The first thing you must do, then, is to place the same recordset on this page as you already placed on the detail page.

Instead of forcing you to rebuild a recordset field by field, UltraDev offers a convenient way to copy an existing recordset from one page to another.

1) Open the product_detail page, select *Recordset(rsProducts)* in the Data Bindings panel, right-click (Windows) or Control+click (Mac), and choose *Copy* from the pop-up menu.

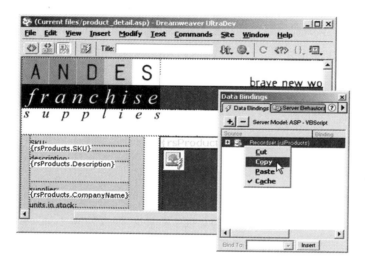

2) Open the product_resultlist page, click inside the Data Bindings panel, right-click (Windows) or Control+click (Mac), and choose *Paste* from the pop-up menu.

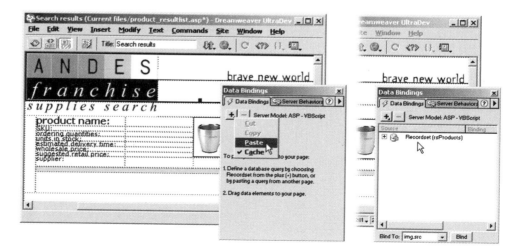

The rsProducts recordset will be copied into the Data Bindings panel of the product_result page.

TIP *In addition to the right-click method, you also can copy and paste recordsets by clicking the right-pointing arrow in the Data Bindings panel's top-right corner and using the drop-down menu.*

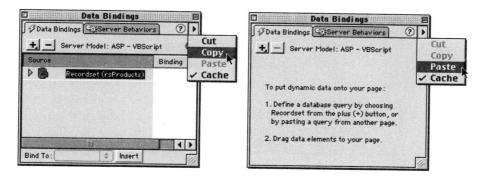

3) Click the + next to *Recordset(rsProducts)* in the Data Bindings panel to expand the recordset.

You're now ready to bind various fields in the product_resultlist page to the rsProducts recordset.

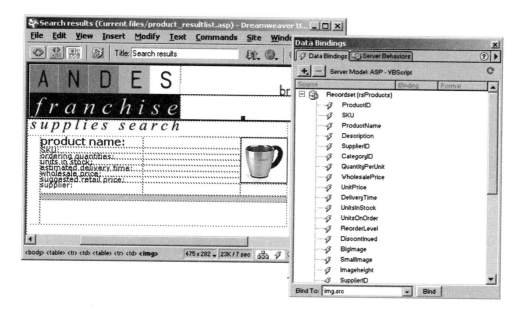

95

4) Using the table below as a guide, insert these seven recordset fields into the product_resultlist page and format accordingly: ProductName, SKU, QuantityPerUnit, UnitsInStock, DeliveryTime, WholesalePrice, UnitPrice, and CompanyName.

PLACEMENT OF DATA IN PRODUCT_DETAIL

LABEL ON PAGE	RECORDSET FIELD NAMES	FORMAT
product name:	ProductName	articletitle (from CSS panel)
SKU	SKU	None
Ordering quantities	QuantityPerUnit	None
units in stock:	UnitsInStock	Number (rounded integer)
estimated delivery time	DeliveryTime	None
wholesale price:	WholesalePrice	Currency (2 decimal places)
suggested retail price:	UnitPrice	Currency (2 decimal places)
supplier:	CompanyName	None

5) Select the image, click the _SmallImage_ field in the Data Bindings panel and click the _Bind_ button.

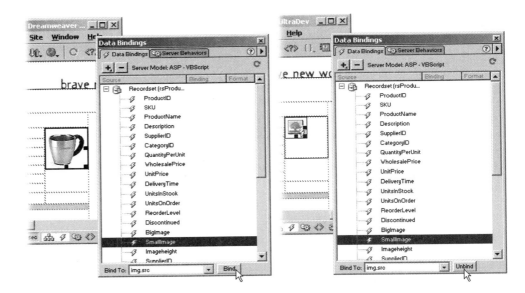

The page's original image will be replaced by the dynamic image icon. The page should now look like so:

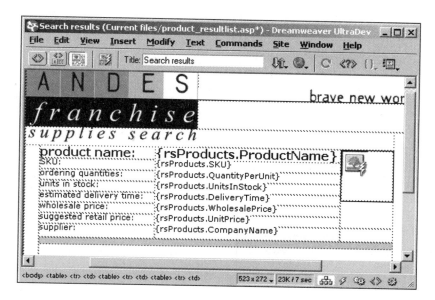

6) **Save the product_resultlist page and click the Live Data View button to see the page with the actual data in place.**

The page now displays the desired information, plus a picture, for a single product. In the next task, you learn how to repeat this same set of fields down the page so that you can display multiple products.

REPEATING REGIONS OF A PAGE

Because this is an abbreviated product listing, it makes sense to fit more than one product on the page. That way, the user has to browse less before finding a particular product of interest. UltraDev has a special server behavior called Repeat Region that repeats a section of a dynamic page as many times as you choose.

1) Use the tag selector at the lower left of the design screen to select the *<table>* tag for the region you want to repeat.

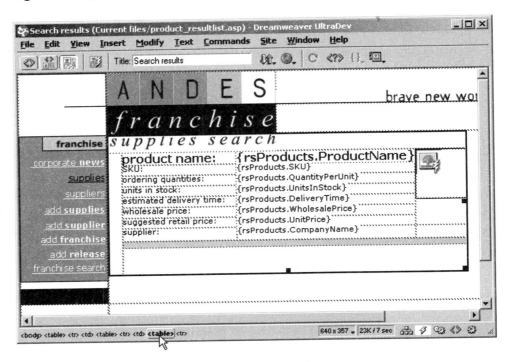

There are several nested tables on the page—click on the tag for the one that displays a bold line around label, product, and image cells.

2) Click the + button in the Server Behaviors panel and choose *Repeat Region* from the drop-down menu.

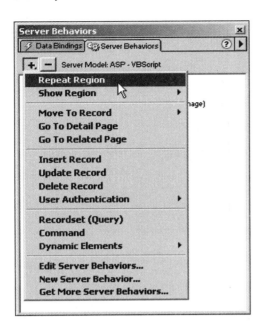

3) When the Repeat Region dialog box appears, replace the 10 with a 5 in the *Records* window. Click *OK*.

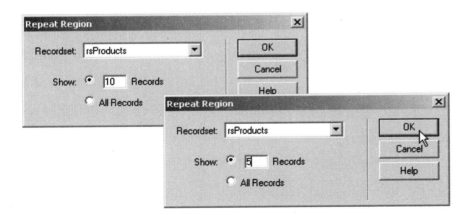

The dialog box will close and the region to be repeated will appear grayed out in the product_resultlist page.

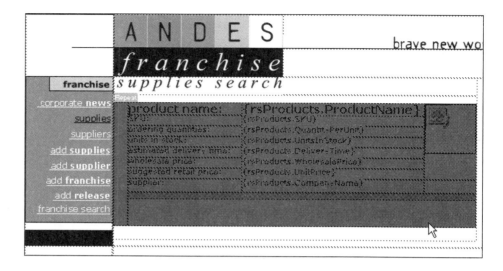

4) **Click the page's Live Data View button to check its appearance with actual data.**

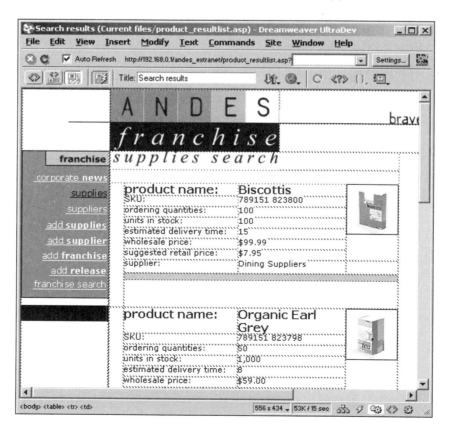

The Live Data View should show the originally selected table repeating five times down the page—with a new product in each repeated region.

5) Save the page, click the page's File Management button, and choose Put (Ctrl+Shift+U Windows, Command+Shift+U Mac) to move the file to the Remote Server. Click *Yes* when asked if you want to include dependent files.

6) Click the Preview in Browser button (F12).

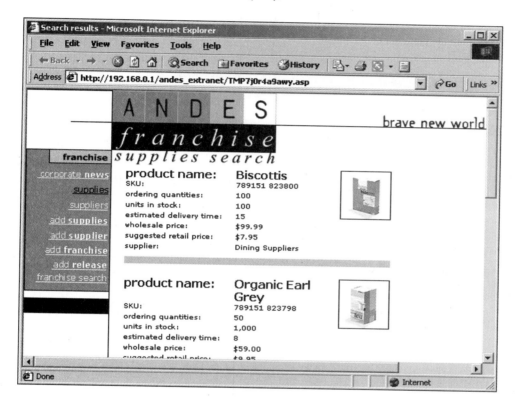

Your browser will display the first five products in the recordset.

ADDING NAVIGATION BUTTONS

In Lesson 4, you used the Recordset Navigation Bar live object to place instant navigation behaviors on the product_detail page. You'll get more insight into UltraDev's server behaviors by creating your own navigation bar, so that's the next task.

1) **Within your site's _Local Folder_, look in the _images_ folder for these four navigation GIFs: _frm-first.gif_, _frm-previous.gif_, _frm-next.gif_, and _frm-last.gif_.**

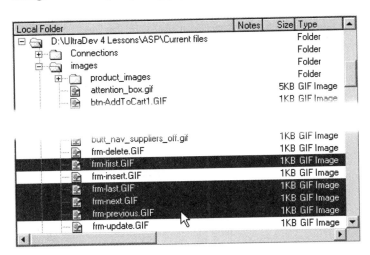

2) **Arrange them in a row at the base of the result_List page, outside the repeat region.**

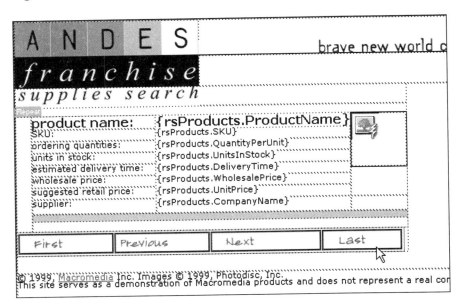

While this example uses a table row to position the buttons, you could also create a layer and position it to appear in the same place on the page.

3) Select the *First* button, click the + button in the Server Behaviors panel, and choose *Move To Record > Move To First Record*.

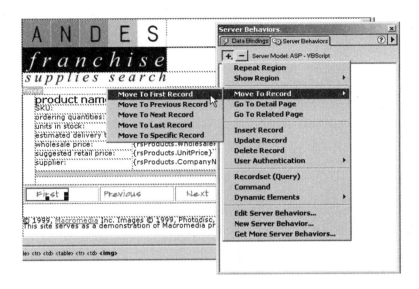

4) Click *OK* in the Move To First Record dialog box that appears.

The page's *First* button will turn gray, indicating that a server behavior has been applied to the image. In this case, the behavior will trigger the display of the first set of records. That set will contain five products because that's what you specified in the Repeating Regions of a Page task.

5) With the *First* button still selected, click the + button in the Server Behaviors panel, and choose *Show Region > Show Region If Not First Record*.

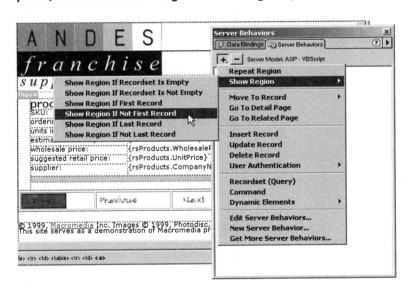

A small *Show If* tag will be attached to the First button, indicating that a conditional behavior has been bound to the image. This behavior dictates that the First button will appear only when the page doesn't contain the first record. That makes sense, when you think about it, since the user won't need the *First* button if the page with the first record is visible. This same basic display "if not" behavior will be used to control the display of the other navigation buttons as well.

6) Select the *Previous* button. Repeat steps 3–5, except in step 3 choose *Move to Previous Record* from the drop-down menu. In step 5, choose *Show Region If Not First Record*.

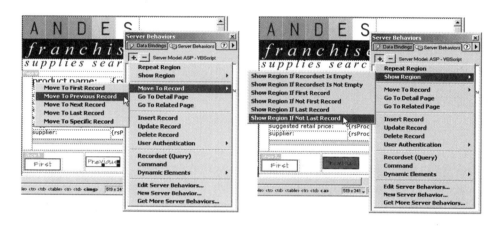

These two behaviors will be attached to the *Previous* button. The Show Region If Not First Record is used because there's no reason for the *Previous* button to appear if the first page of records is being displayed.

7) Select the *Next* button. Repeat steps 3–5, except choose *Move to Next Record* in step 3 and choose *Show Region If Not Last Record* in step 5.

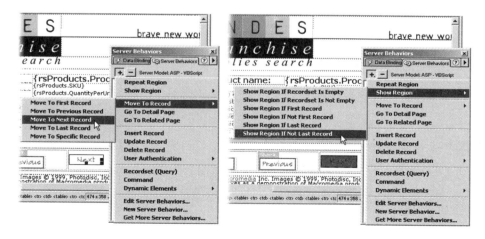

8) Select the *Last* button. Repeat steps 3–5, except choose *Move to Last Record* in step 3 and choose *Show Region If Not Last Record* in step 5.

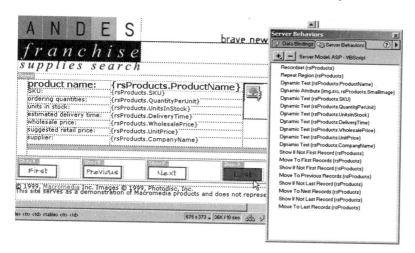

Each of the four navigation buttons now has two server behaviors attached, which are listed in the Server Behaviors panel.

9) Save the page, click the page's File Management button, and choose Put (Ctrl+Shift+U Windows, Command+Shift+U Mac) to move the file to the Remote Server. Click *Yes* when asked if you want to include dependent files.

10) Click the Preview in Browser button (F12).

The first set of five products will appear in your browser. Scroll to the bottom and you'll see that the *First* and *Previous* buttons are hidden, which is exactly what you want.

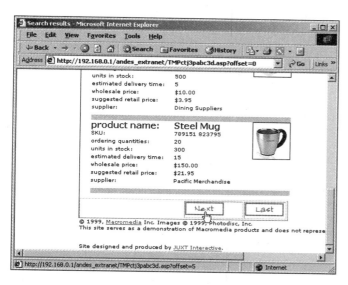

11) Click the *Next* button in the browser.

The second set of five products appears and if you scroll to the bottom, you'll see all four navigation buttons, which makes sense since you're in the middle of the products.

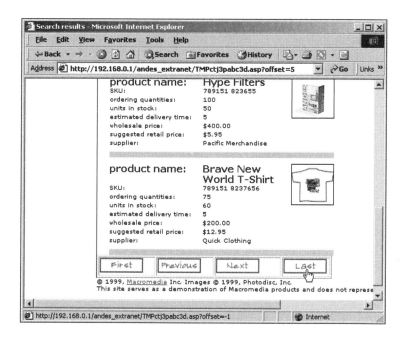

12) Click the *Last* button in the browser.

Again, scroll to the bottom and you'll see just the *First* and *Previous* buttons since you are at the end of the product listings.

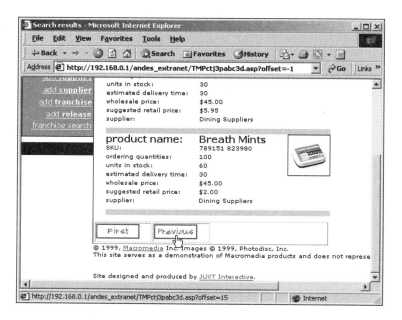

ADDING A NAVIGATION STATUS DISPLAY

Users browsing through a large database like to know where they are in the whole scheme of things. An onscreen display that says something like "Products 11 –16 of 212" can be very helpful. This type of display is known as a navigation status display, and UltraDev has a live object that lets you quickly create such a display. You're going to drop this object onto the product_resultlist page. Your work will be easier if you switch to the Live Data View instead of staying in the Design View.

1) Open the product_resultlist page, place your cursor in the empty design area to the right of the *supplies search* header and insert a carriage return to give yourself some space.

2) Open the CSS Styles panel (Shift+F11) and select the *newlist* style.

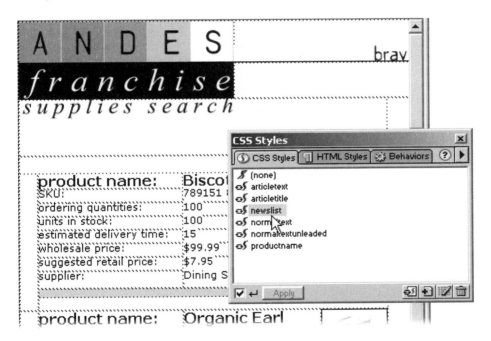

3) With the Objects panel visible (Ctrl+F2 Windows, Command+F2 Mac), select *Live* from the drop-down, and click the Recordset Navigation Status icon.

4) Click *OK* in the dialog box that appears.

A complete navigation status line appears at the insertion point. The information it displays makes it clear to users where they are relative to the rest of the records.

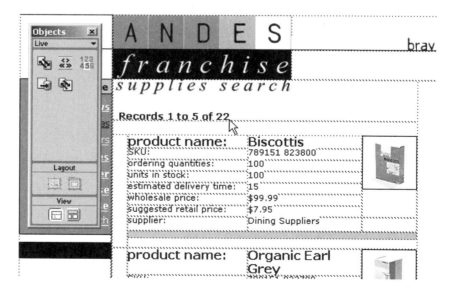

5) Save the page and click the Preview in Browser button (F12).

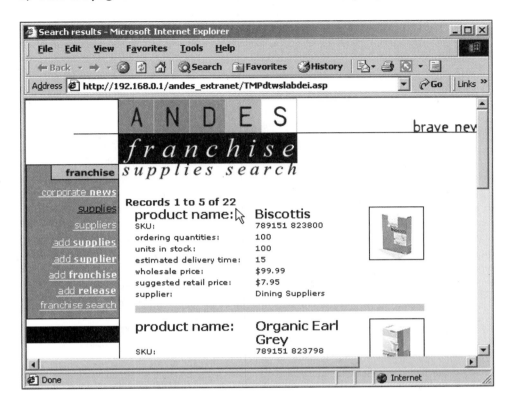

The same set of records will appear within your browser. Use the navigation buttons at the bottom of the page to move around and see how the navigation status line changes in turn. Now you have a way for users to browse the complete catalog five items at a time, seeing a thumbnail image of each product, and just enough information to know if the product is of interest. Next you need to give them a hyperlink so they can click and go to the detail page for any product.

LINKING A RESULTS LIST TO A DETAILS PAGE

In linking a results list to a details page, you cannot simply hyperlink a product name to a individual product page. That's because the products displayed on the results list change as users browse through it. Instead, an index of the product the user clicked must be transferred in a query string, so that the detail page knows which record to load.

To make this work correctly takes two stages: first you need to create the query string on the results page; then you need to set up the detail page to respond to it.

1) With the product_resultlist page still open, click the Live Data View button to switch back to the Design View.

2) Select the placeholder for the product name _{rsProducts.ProductName}_, click the + button in the Server Behaviors panel, and choose _Go To Detail Page_.

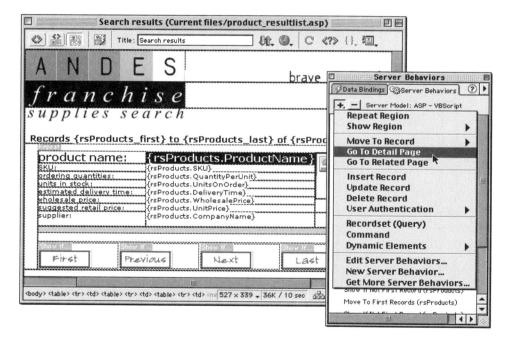

3) When the Go To Detail dialog box opens, click the *Browse* button, navigate to the product_detail page, and open it.

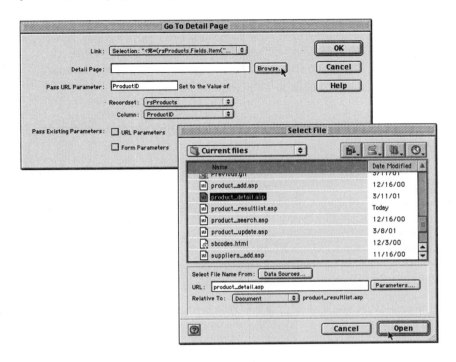

4) When the Go To Detail Page dialog box reappears, select *ProductID* in the *Pass URL Parameter* window and replace it by typing in id**. Click *OK* to close the dialog box.**

111

This way, if the user clicks a product whose index is 5, the query string will be id=5. Make sure that both of the *Pass Existing Parameters* boxes (*URL Parameters* and *Form Parameters*) remain unchecked.

5) Save the page, click the page's File Management button, and choose Put (Ctrl+Shift+U Windows, Command+Shift+U Mac) to move the file to the Remote Server. Click *Yes* when asked if you want to include dependent files.

6) Open the product_detail page, click the + button in the Server Behaviors panel, and choose *Move To Record > Move To Specific Record*.

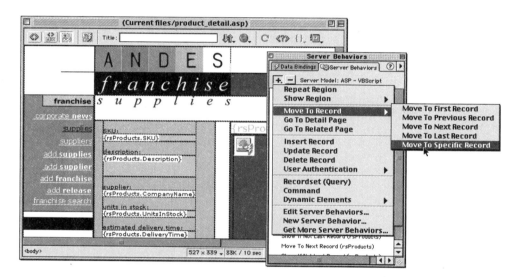

7) Click *OK* when the Move To Specific Record dialog box appears.

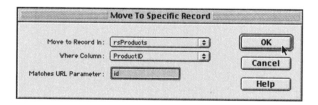

These two steps complete the dynamic linking between the resultlist and detail pages.

8) Save the page, click the page's File Management button, and choose Put (Ctrl+Shift+U Windows, Command+Shift+U Mac) to move the file to the Remote Server. Click *Yes* when asked if you want to include dependent files.

9) Switch back to the product_resultlist page and click the Preview in Browser button (F12).

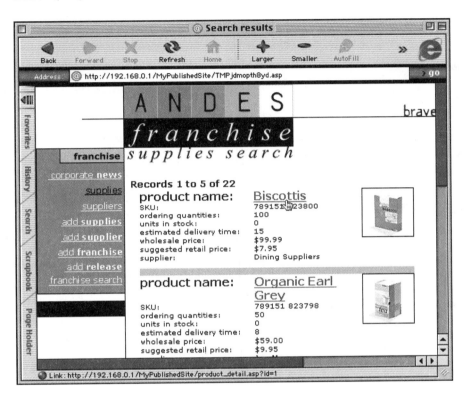

When the browser opens, each product name in the resultslist page will include a link to that particular product's detail page.

10) Click any hyperlinked product name.

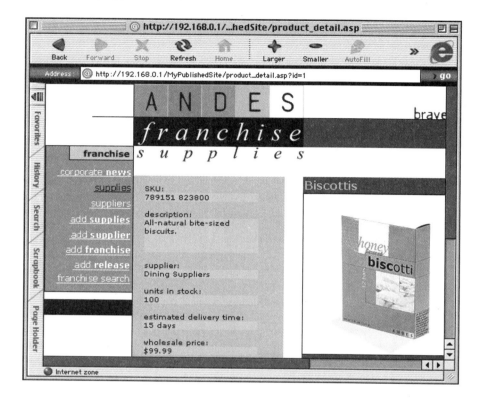

The link automatically takes your browser to the detail page for that product.

WHAT YOU HAVE LEARNED

In this lesson, you have:

- Copied a recordset from one page to another, preserving all the field data and without having to rebuild the recordset by hand (pages 94–97)

- Repeated a dynamic region of a page by using the Repeat Region server behavior (pages 98–101)

- Created a live navigation bar, associated a set of server behaviors with different parts of the bar, and then added the bar to a page (pages 101–106)

- Added a dynamic navigation status text to a results page, enabling browsers to see where they are relative to all the records (pages 107–109)

- Dynamically linked every product listed in a results page to its own page of detailed information (pages 110–114)

building insert pages

LESSON 6

Like all merchandising companies, Andes Coffee does not stay still. New products come along, and old products change their specifications. When the time comes to add a new product, a new record could, of course, be added to the database table by using Microsoft Access. However, many small to mid-size companies find it just as convenient to enter new data via the Web by filling out an online form on what's known as an insert page. In this lesson, you will use UltraDev to add a new product, Andes Carob Bars, to the database.

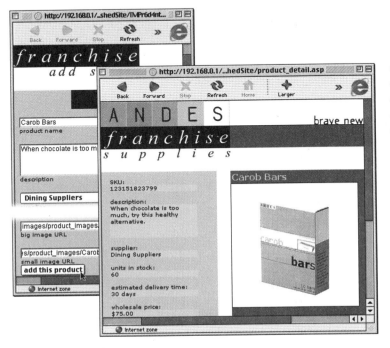

By building UltraDev insert pages, you can use a Web browser to update records (left) and have the changes reflected in all your site's pages (right).

You will create the insert page in two ways: first using the special live object that does everything at once, but with very limited design capability, and then again field by field in a fully designed page following the Andes Coffee corporate design.

In the course of building the insert page, you'll get more practice in using text input fields, multiline input fields, radio buttons, drop-down menus, and hidden fields.

WHAT YOU WILL LEARN

In this lesson, you will:

- Create an insert page using a live object
- Add a hidden field to a page
- Create an insert page field by field
- Add a new record using the insert page
- Check the insert form using validation behaviors

APPROXIMATE TIME

This lesson takes approximately one hour to complete.

LESSON FILES

Media Files:

none

Beginning Files:

UltraDev 4 Lessons\...\Current files\product_detail

UltraDev 4 Lessons\...\Current files\product_add

UltraDev 4 Lessons\...\Current files\product_search

Completed Files:

Same as Beginning Files, plus product_add_live_object

CREATING A NEW RECORDSET

Because the Record Insertion Form will include a list menu, you first need to create a new page with a new recordset.

1) Create a new page by choosing File > New (Ctrl+N Windows, Command+N Mac), name it *product_add_live_object*, and save it to your site. Create a new recordset by clicking the + button in either the Data Bindings or Server Behaviors panel and choosing *Recordset(Query)* from the drop-down menu.

2) Name the new recordset *rsSuppliers*, choose *connAndes* as the *Connection* and *Suppliers* as the *Table*. Choose the *Selected* radio button and select the *SupplierID* and *CompanyName* fields from the list:

If the dialog box opens with advanced form displayed, switch to the simple form by clicking the *Simple* button. (If the *Advanced* button appears, you're already in the simple form.)

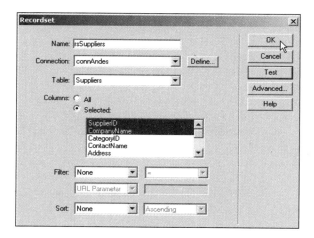

3) Click *Test* in the Recordset dialog box.

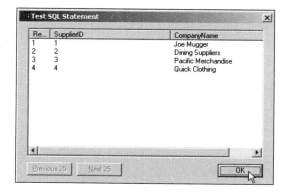

The test statement will display the recordset's four suppliers and their corresponding IDs.

4) Click *OK* to close the dialog box.

The rsSuppliers recordset will be added to the Data Bindings panel. Now that you've created a new page and its accompanying recordset, you're ready to add a live object to it.

CREATING AN INSERT PAGE WITH A LIVE OBJECT

The Record Insertion Form live object uses a single, comprehensive dialog box to set up a whole array of fields, create a page for them, insert the records, and redirect users to the home page. It's an ingenious feature—but the dialog box requires some concentration to get everything right.

1) With the product_add_live_object page still open, give it a title by typing Add new product **into the *Title* window. Choose *Live* from the Objects panel's drop-down menu, then click the Insert Record Insertion Form icon.**

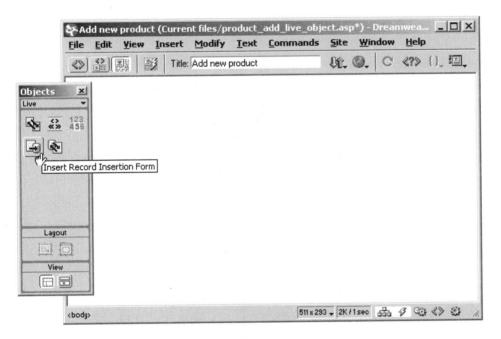

The Insert Record Insertion Form dialog box will open.

2) Choose *connAndes* as the *Connection* and *Products* as the *Insert Into Table* target. Then click the *Browse* button to the right of the *After Inserting, Go To* text field.

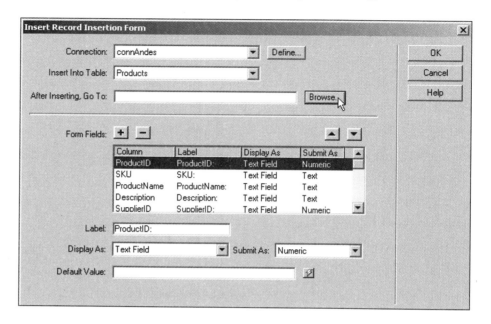

3) Use the Select File dialog box to navigate to your site's Current files folder and select the *product_search* page.

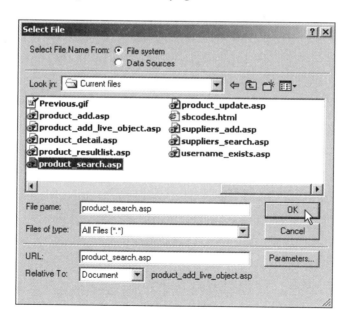

Users are redirected to this page after they insert new records.

4) Click *OK*.

The Insert Record Insertion Form dialog box will reappear. The next step will be to delete several lines.

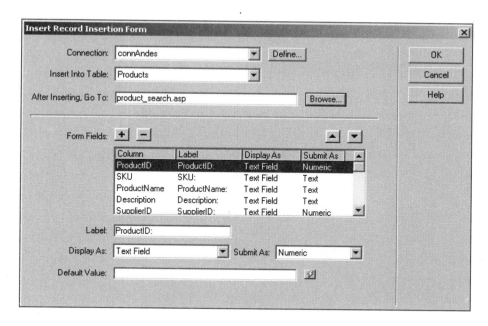

NOTE *Take a moment to study the dialog box's* Form Fields *list and the* Label, Display As, Submit As, *and* Default Value *boxes beneath it. Initially, the dialog box simply extracts the name and data type of every field in the targeted data table (*Products, *in this case) and lists each one's field name, screen label, display type, and data type.*

By selecting a line (a data field) in the Form Fields *list, you can use the four boxes beneath to edit the field's* Label, Display As, *and* Submit As *values. The* Default Value, *if any, can be bound to dynamic data (such as a server variable or a field from a different data table) by clicking the lightning bolt. The + and – buttons above the* Form Fields *list let you add and delete lines; the up and down arrow buttons let you change the list order.*

5) Select the *ProductID* item in the *Form Fields* list and click the – button to delete it.

This item, which won't be needed on the page, will disappear from the *Form Fields* list and the next item will be automatically selected.

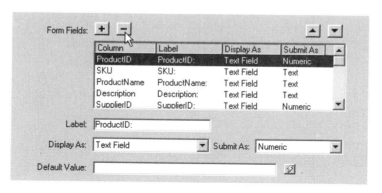

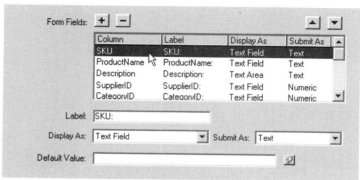

6) Repeat step 6 to delete four other unneeded items: *UnitsOnOrder*, *ReorderLevel*, *Discontinued*, and *Imageheight*.

The Imageheight item actually will be needed as a hidden field, but this dialog box can't handle that so it will be added back in later. There are four other items that need editing. Use the table as a guide.

DATA FIELDS IN THE PRODUCTS DATA TABLE

DATA FIELD NAME	FORM ELEMENT	PAGE LABEL
Description	Text area	Description
SupplierID	Menu	Supplier
CategoryID	Radio group	Category
QuantityPerUnit	Text input	Ordering quantities

7) Select the *Description* item, then click the *Display As* drop-down menu, and choose *Text Area*.

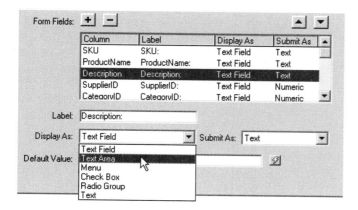

The *Text Area* choice will create a text window that's 50 characters wide by 5 lines deep.

8) Select the *SupplierID* item in the *Form Fields* list, change its label to *Supplier:* in the *Label* text field, and choose *Menu* from the *Display As* drop-down menu.

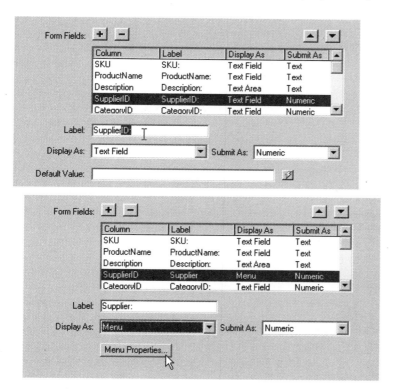

9) Click the *Menu Properties* button to reach the Menu Properties dialog box.

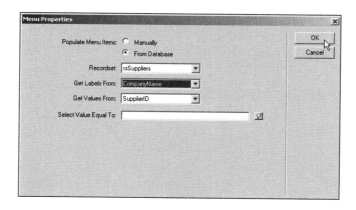

10) Select the *From Database* radio button, then set the *Get Labels From* menu to *CompanyName* and the *Get Values From* menu to *SupplierID*. Click *OK* to close the dialog box.

By now you recognize this method of having a page display user-friendly labels while pulling values from another, numbered field.

11) Select the *CategoryID* item, change its label to *Category:* in the *Label* text window, and choose *Radio Group* from the *Display As* drop-down menu.

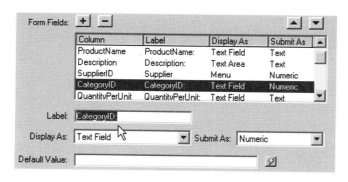

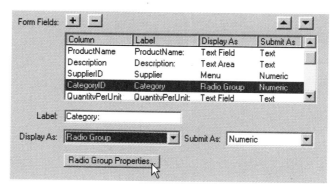

124

12) Click the *Radio Group Properties* button to reach the Radio Group Properties dialog box. Select the *Manually* radio button, replace *button1* with Coffee in the *Label* window, and type 1 into the *Value* window.

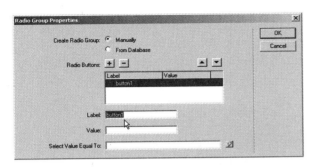

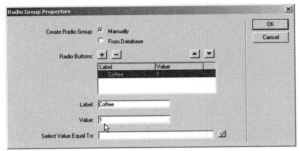

13) Click the + button to create a new label and value and enter Food as the *Label* and 2 as the *Value*. Repeat to add Merch (3) and Clothing (4), then click *OK*.

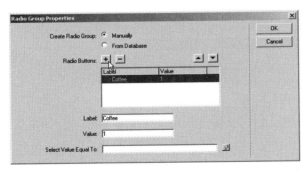

This will create a set of four radio buttons, which share the common name CategoryID. Radio buttons make sense for this field because there are only four possible choices. The labels will appear on the screen beside each radio button, with each having its own value.

14) Select the *QuantityPerUnit* item and change its *Label* to Ordering quantities:, **then change the *WholesalePrice* item's *Label* to** Wholesale price:, **and change the *UnitPrice* items's *Label* to** Suggested retail price:.

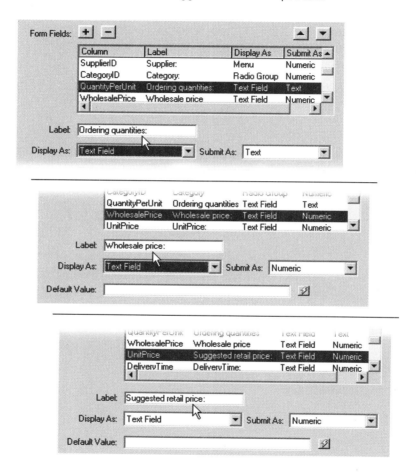

Look over all the items in the Insert Record Insertion Form dialog box, taking care that you have deleted the correct fields and made the necessary changes for the remaining labels and displays.

15) Click *OK* to close the Insert Record Insertion Form dialog box.
The product_add_live_object page will reappear, complete with the record insertion form. However, you still need to add a hidden field before you're done.

ADDING A HIDDEN FIELD

Since the Record Insertion Form has no option for inserting a hidden form field, you need to add one for the Imageheight field and set its value to 1.

1) At the bottom of the product_add_live_object page, place the cursor in the empty table cell to the left of the *Insert Record* button.

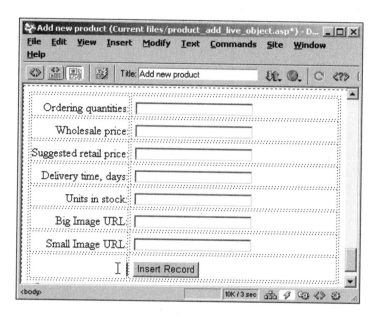

2) Choose *Forms* from the Objects panel's drop-down menu, then click the Insert Hidden Field icon.

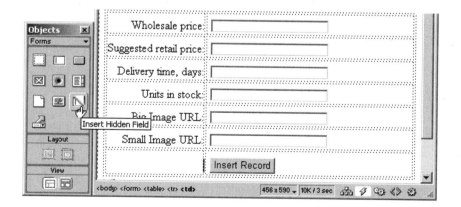

A hidden field object will be inserted into the cell.

3) With the object still selected, open the Property Inspector (Ctrl+F3 Windows, Command+F3 Mac), name the *HiddenField* object *Imageheight*, and type *1* into the *Value* text field.

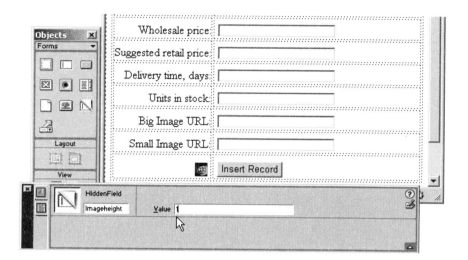

4) Save the page, click the page's File Management button, and choose Put (Ctrl+Shift+U Windows, Command+Shift+U Mac) to move the file to the Remote Server. Click *Yes* when asked if you want to include dependent files.

5) Transfer the product_search page to the Remote Server as well.

You're now ready to use the page's Insert Record button to add records to your database.

USING THE INSERT PAGE

The design of the product_add_live_object page could still be enhanced with such things as headers and logos. However, as you'll see later in this lesson, you gain more design control over insert pages by building them field by field. Instead, the focus here is to show how you can use UltraDev's insert pages to update a database from within a Web browser.

1) Open the product_add_live_object page and click the Preview in Browser button (F12).

The page will open in your default Web browser.

128

2) Fill in each field, using the table below as a guide, and click the *Insert Record* button when you're done.

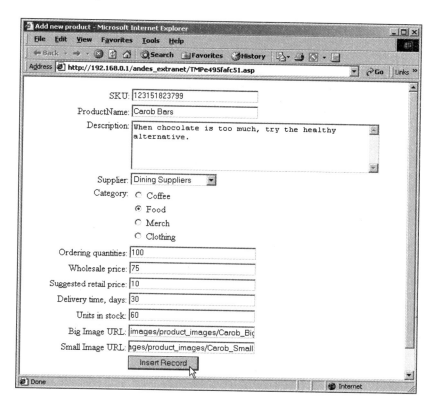

The record will be added to the database. There are several ways to see the additional record for yourself.

NEW RECORD CONTENT FOR INSERT PAGE

FIELD NAME	SUGGESTED CONTENT
ProductName	Carob Bars
Description	[Create your own]
SupplierID	Dining suppliers
SKU	123151823799
CategoryID	Food
QuantityPerUnit	100
UnitsInStock	60
DeliveryTime	30
WholesalePrice	75 (no need for the $sign)
UnitPrice	10 (no need for the $sign)
BigImage	images/product_images/Carob_Big.jpg
SmallImage	images/product_images/Carob_Small.jpg

3) Open the product_detail page within UltraDev and double-click Recordset(*rsProducts*) in the Data Bindings panel.

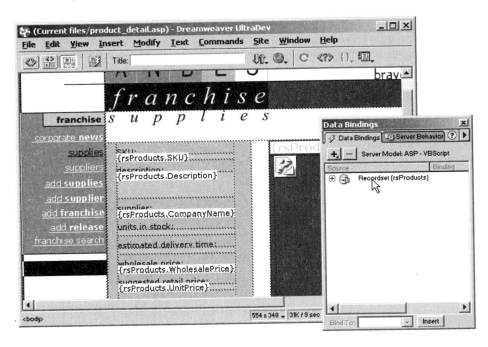

4) Click the *Test* button when the Recordset dialog box opens.

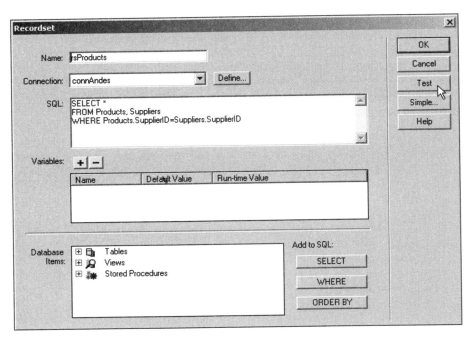

The new Carob Bars product, with its description and other information, will appear as the last record in the Test SQL Statement dialog box. Click *OK* to close the dialog box. You also can use your Web browser to see that the Carob Bar product has been added to the base.

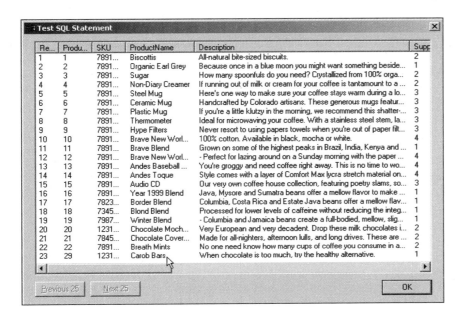

5) **Open the product_resultlist page and click the Preview in Browser button (F12).**

6) **Scroll to the bottom of the page and click the *Last* button.**

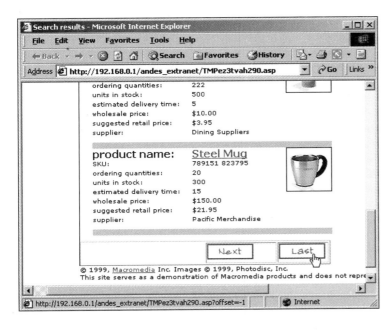

The browser will jump to the last set of product records. Scroll to the bottom and you'll see that the Carob Bars have been added.

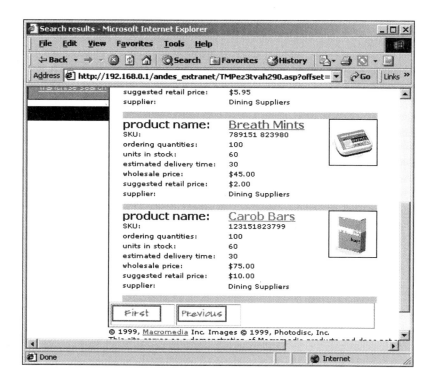

Now you're going to create a page with the same functions as the product_add_ live_object page, but without the support of the live object. This will take longer— in fact the rest of the tasks in this lesson will focus on this page. But the benefit of creating an insert page field by field is that you have more control over the page design.

USING AND INSPECTING TEXT INPUT FIELDS

Text input fields form the backbone of this page, just as they do for most pages. This task shows you how to check to see if they're formatted properly and clearly named.

1) Open the product_add page.

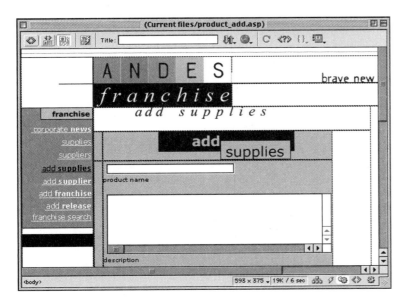

This page provides a skeleton for the insert page you'll be building for the rest of the lesson. You'll start by verifying the names of the text input fields already on the page.

2) Select the *product name* field, open the Property Inspector (Ctrl+F3 Windows, Command+F3 Mac), and check that *Type* is set to *Single line* and that the name in the text field roughly corresponds to the field's page label.

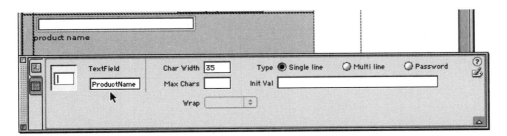

The text field's name (in the inspector's text field) and the field label appearing on the page do not have to exactly match. For example, *ProductName* and *product name* are fine. The point is simply to label the field clearly enough that you'll not get confused.

3) Use the Property Inspector to check that the following eight fields also are set to *Single line* and clearly named: *SKU, ordering quantities, units in stock, estimated delivery time, wholesale price, suggested retail price, big image URL,* and *small image URL.*

While all eight are formatted correctly, the point here is to make a habit of using the Property Inspector to verify the formatting of your fields when building an insert page by hand.

TIP *You also can open the Property Inspector by right+clicking (Windows) or Control+ clicking (Macintosh) any field.*

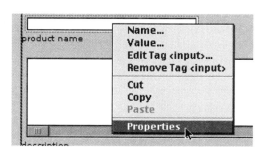

4) Select the description field and use the Property Inspector to make sure that *Type* is set to *Multi line*.

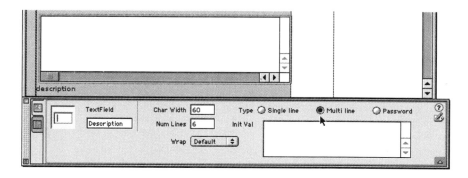

The 60-character-by-6-line multi line element ensures that there's plenty of space to describe a product.

USING RADIO BUTTONS

The product_add page's Product Category field lends itself to the use of a radio button group since you want to offer users just four choices.

1) Select the *Category* text input field and delete it.

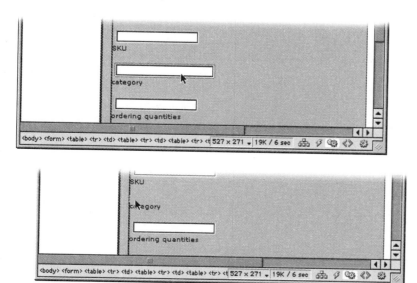

2) Select Forms from the Objects panel's drop-down menu, then click the Radio Box icon four times to add four buttons.

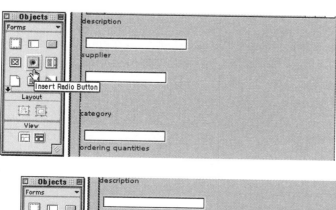

3) Use the Property Inspector to name each button *CategoryID* and, from left to right, give each a value of *1*, *2*, *3*, and *4*.

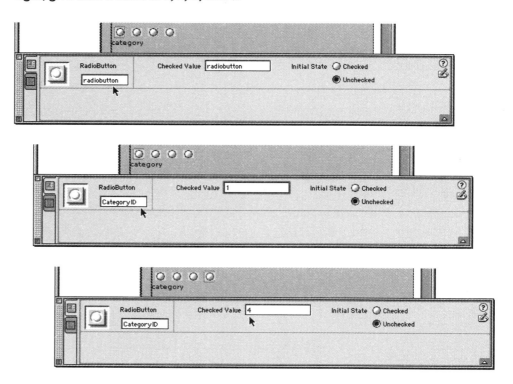

By naming each button the same thing—*CategoryID*—you create a single group, even though each button has a different value.

4) From left to right, type on the page labels for each button of *coffee, food, merch,* and *clothing*.

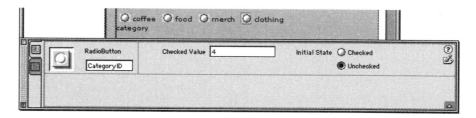

Your page now has a radio button group. The next task will be to add a drop-down menu and populate it from a recordset.

NOTE *There's no need to use server behaviors for these dynamic radio buttons because there's no default value to fetch from the recordset. You can see this by looking in the Property Inspector where the* Initial State *for each button is* Unchecked.

USING MENUS

A drop-down menu is the ideal form element for specifying the supplier of a new product—assuming that the supplier is an existing supplier and not a new one requiring its own insert page. The reason for using a menu is that the data table expects just an ID number for the supplier, whereas the user of this page would obviously prefer to select by the more easily recognized company name. Just as you learned in Lesson 4, the game here is to set up a selection list consisting of the suppliers' company names and using their corresponding IDs as values.

1) Click the *⟨form⟩* tag in the product_add page's tag selector, and type Andes Insert **in the** Form Name **text window of the Property Inspector panel.**

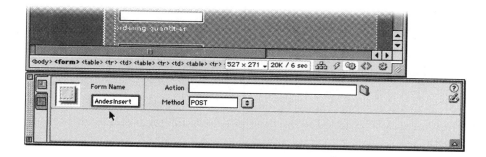

2) Open the product_add_live_object page and select Recordset*(rsSuppliers)* in the Data Bindings panel, right+click (Windows) or Control+click (Macintosh), and choose *Copy* from the pop-up menu.

3) Switch back to the product_add page, click inside the Data Bindings panel, right+click (Windows) or Control+click (Macintosh), and choose *Paste* from the pop-up menu.

The recordset will be copied to the product_add page. This is exactly the technique you learned in Lesson 5.

4) **Select the *supplier* text input field in the product_add page and delete it.**

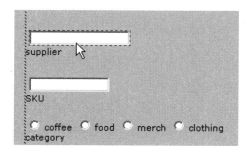 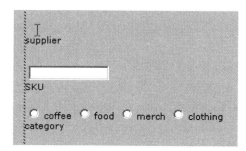

5) **Select *Forms* from the Objects panel's drop-down menu, then click the Insert List/Menu icon.**

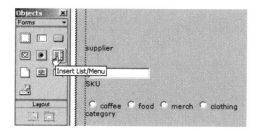 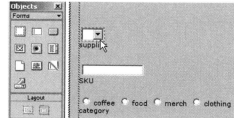

A drop-down menu will be added to the page just above the *supplier* label. Make sure that *Menu* is checked as the *Type* in the Property Inspector.

6) **With the menu still selected, type** SupplierID **in the *List/Menu* text window of the Property Inspector panel.**

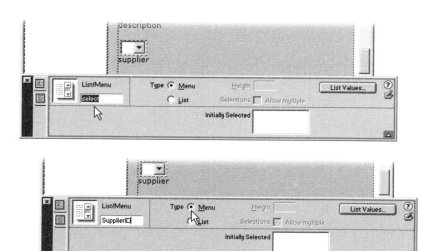

7) With the menu still selected, click the + button in the Server Behaviors panel and choose *Dynamic Elements* > *Dynamic List*/Menu.

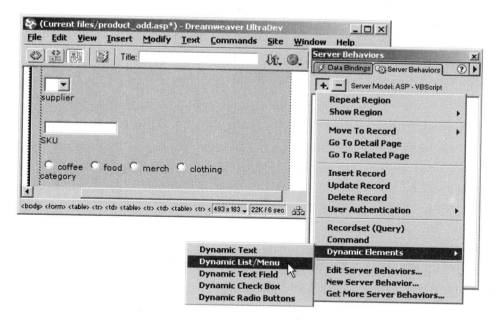

The Dynamic List/Menu dialog box will open.

8) Choose *CompanyName* from the *Get Labels From* drop-down menu and click *OK* to close the dialog box.

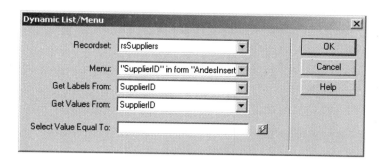

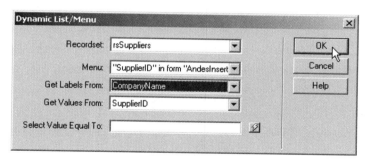

139

9) With the menu still selected, click the *List Values* button in the Property Inspector.

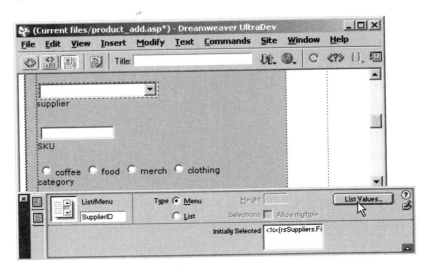

The List Values dialog box will open.

10) Click the + button, type Select a supplier **into the blank *Item Label* text window, and type** 0 **(zero) into the blank *Value* text window. Click the up arrow to move the new line to the top of the list.**

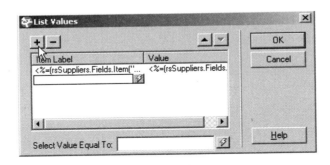

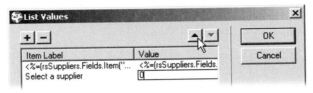

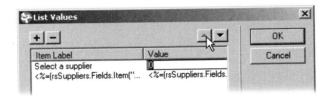

140

Use the Tab key to jump from the *Item Label* window to the *Value* window.

11) Click *OK* to close the dialog box.

This will make *Select a supplier* the menu's default value—in effect, using the menu as a prompt for users to make a choice. Let's take a look.

12) Save the page, click the page's File Management button, and choose Put (Ctrl+Shift+U Windows, Command+Shift+U Mac) to move the file to the Remote Server. Click *Yes* when asked if you want to include dependent files.

13) Click the Preview in Browser button (F12).

When the page appears in your Web browser, the supplier menu will display the *Select a supplier* prompt. You're not quite ready, however, to start adding new products.

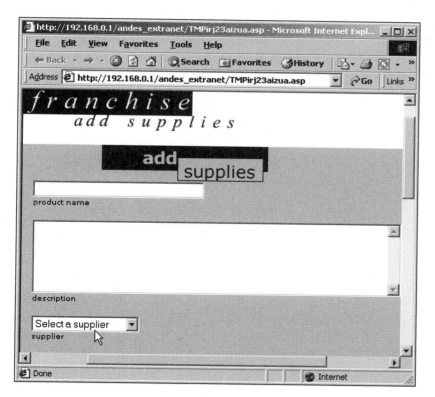

INSERTING THE NEW RECORD

Now that you've completed the design of your insert page, you need to attach the server behavior that will actually insert the record into the recordset.

1) With the product_add page open, click the + button in the Server Behaviors panel, and choose *Insert Record*.

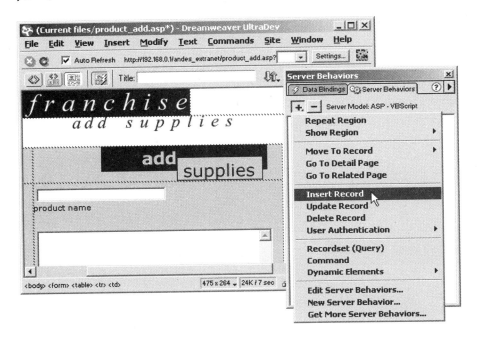

The Insert Record dialog box will open.

2) Choose *connAndes* as the *Connection* and *Products* as the *Table*, then click *Browse* to select your site's product_search page as the *After Inserting, Go To* target page.

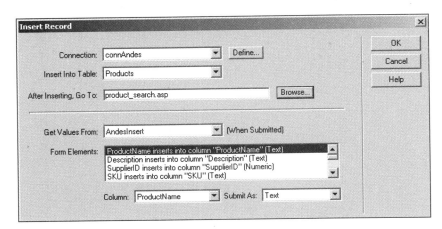

3) Scroll through the *Form Elements* list, making sure that the correct element matches up with the right column. If need be, use the *Column* and *Submit As* drop-down menus to edit incorrect lines.

4) When all the elements are correct, click *OK* to close the dialog box.

5) Save the page, click the page's File Management button, and choose Put (Ctrl+Shift+U Windows, Command+Shift+U Mac) to move the file to the Remote Server. Click *Yes* when asked if you want to include dependent files.

6) Click the Preview in Browser button (F12), add a product to your recordset, and click the *add this product* button.

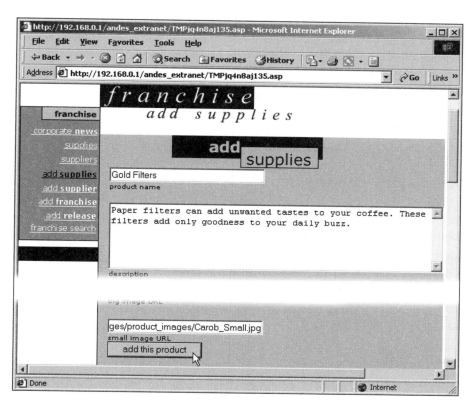

Make up your own product, using the same path and images you used for the carob bars: images/product_images/Carob_Big.jpg and images/product_images/Carob_Small.jpg.

CHECKING THE FORM WITH VALIDATION BEHAVIORS

To make this a fully professional form, you should add validation behaviors to it. Validation uses client-side JavaScript to prevent a form from being submitted if it has not been filled out completely or correctly. UltraDev provides a dialog box for you to define which fields you want to require users to fill out and any formatting restrictions you want to impose.

1) Choose Window > Behaviors (Shift+F3) to open the Behaviors palette. With the product_add page still open, click the *add this product* button to select it.

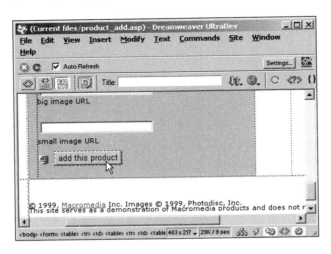

2) *Click* the + button in the Behaviors panel and choose *Validate Form* from the drop-down menu.

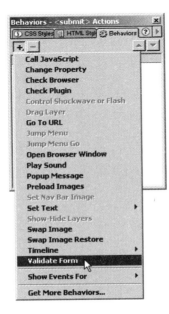

Make sure to use the *Behaviors* panel, not the *Server Behaviors* panel. The Validate Form dialog box will open.

3) Scroll through the *Named Fields* list and use the *Value checkbox* and *Accept* radio buttons to impose restrictions on the fields. Use the table below as a guide in setting required fields and formats.

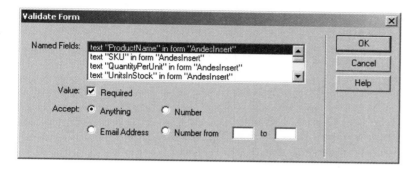

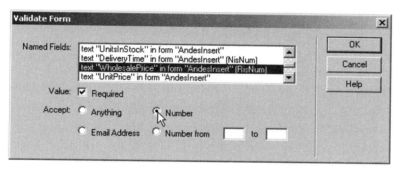

VALIDATION REQUIREMENTS FOR THE INSERT PAGE

FIELD	REQUIRED	ACCEPT
SKU	Y	Anything
ProductName	Y	Anything
Description	Y	Anything
QuantityPerUnit	N	
WholesalePrice	Y	Number
UnitPrice	N	
DeliveryTime	Y	Anything
UnitsInStock	N	
BigImage	Y	Anything
SmallImage	Y	Anything

4) Click *OK* to close the dialog box when you're done.

The validation behavior will be added to the Behavior panel.

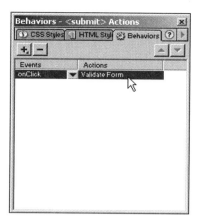

LINKING TO THE INSERT PAGE

The last step in making your insert page useful is to create a link to it from the product_detail page. This link will also be used in later lessons.

1) Open the product_detail page, scroll to the bottom, and click in the *blank* area below the *{rsProducts.UnitPrice}* field. Use the Insert Image icon in the Common Objects palette to select the *frm-insert.gif* in your local site's images folder.

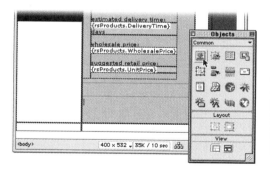
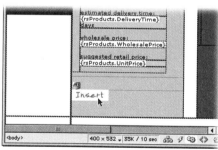

2) With *frm-insert.gif* still selected, open the Property Inspector (Ctrl+F3 Windows, Command+F3 Mac) and use the Link window's icons to navigate to the product_add page.

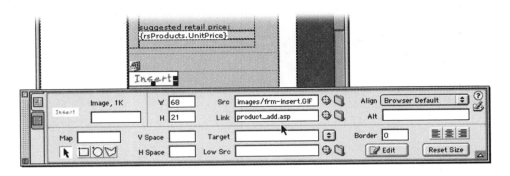

The Insert gif will be linked to the product_add page

WHAT YOU HAVE LEARNED

In this lesson, you have:

- Used UltraDev's Record Insertion Form live object to create an insert page that lets users add records to a database via a Web browser (pages 119–126)

- Added a hidden form field to the insert page, using the Object panel's Forms panel (pages 127–128)

- Created an insert page from scratch, adding text input fields, radio button groups, and drop-down menus (pages 128–141)

- Used the newly created insert page to add records to the recordset via a Web browser (pages 142–143)

- Added JavaScript-based form validation behaviors to the insert page and used them to control and format submissions (pages 144–146)

building update pages

Update pages bring all the details of a selected product into a form, where they can be edited within a Web browser. UltraDev's Update Record server behavior then overwrites the record in the database with the revised product information.

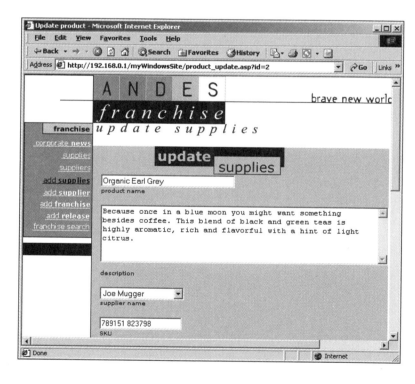

Although it's not much to look at, the update page puts all the text from a product detail page into editable fields, which can be updated at the click of a button.

In this lesson, you will learn to use the Record Update Form live object. Then you'll complete the product_update page that you worked on in Lesson 4, link it to the product_detail page, and add the server behavior to actually edit the database when the page is submitted.

Just as you did in Lesson 6, first you will create an instant page with a live object and then revert to the update page designed in the Andes corporate style to complete that page manually.

WHAT YOU WILL LEARN

In this lesson, you will:

- Create an update page by using a live object
- Create an update page field by field
- Complete input fields for the update page
- Apply the update server behavior to the update page

APPROXIMATE TIME

It usually takes about 45 minutes to complete this lesson.

LESSON FILES

Media Files:

None

Starting Files:

UltraDev 4 Lessons\...\Current files\product_update

UltraDev 4 Lessons\...\Current files\product_add

UltraDev 4 Lessons\...\Current files\product_detail

UltraDev 4 Lessons\...\Current files\product_resultlist

Completed Project:

Same as Starting Files, plus product_update_live_object

CREATING AN UPDATE PAGE

As you learned in Lesson 6, you have to create a fresh page to use a live object.

1) Create a new page by choosing File › New (Ctrl+N Windows, Command+N Macintosh), name it *product_update_live_object*, and save it to your site.

Unlike an insert page, an update page needs a recordset representing the entire Products data table. You'll also need recordsets representing the *SupplierID* and *CompanyName* fields of the Suppliers data table, and a third recordset representing the *CategoryID* and *CategoryName* fields of the Categories data table.

2) Copy the rsSuppliers recordset from the product_add page and the rsUpdate and rsCategories recordsets from the product_update page.

Use the right-click (Control+click on the Macintosh) trick you learned in Lesson 5 to copy the three recordsets and paste them into the new page's Data Bindings panel.

3) Type *Update Product* in the page's *Title* text window, and resave the page.

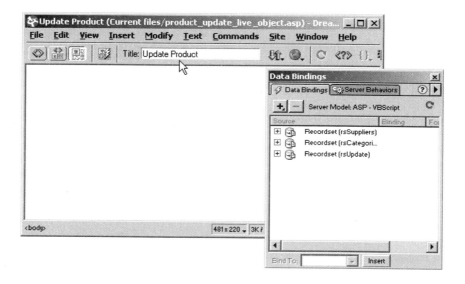

BUILDING AN UPDATE PAGE WITH A LIVE OBJECT

Having used the Record Insertion Form in Lesson 6, you will find this process familiar—except this time you'll be using the Insert Record Update Form.

1) With the product_update_live_object page open, choose *Live* from the Objects palette's drop-down menu, and click the *Insert Record Update Form* icon.

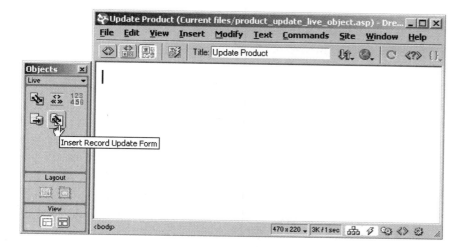

The Insert Record Update Form dialog box opens.

2) Using the drop-down menus, choose *connAndes* as the *Connection*, *Products* as the *Table to Update*, and *rsUpdate* for *Select Record From*. Then click the *Browse* button next to the *After Updating, Go To* text box, and select your site's product_search page.

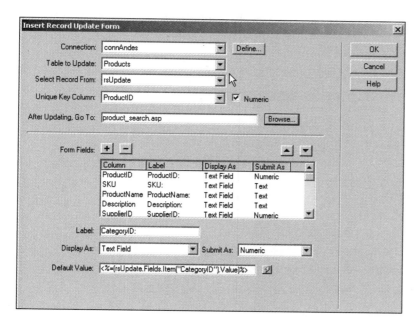

The Unique Key Column text window will be filled in automatically.

3) Select the *ProductID* and *Imageheight* items in the *Form Fields* list, and delete them using the – button.

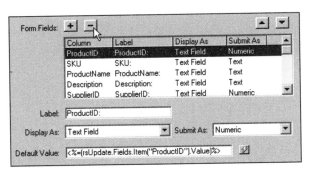

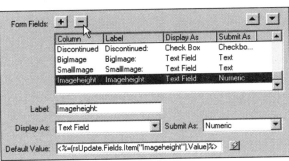

4) Select the *ProductName* item in the *Form Fields* list, and in the *Label* text box, change its label to Product Name:**. Add spaces to any other item labels as needed.**

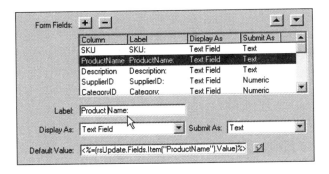

Users depend on clear labels when browsing, so it's best not to use the cryptically named recordset column names. Adding spaces to UnitsInStock, for example, makes your labels more user-friendly.

5) Select the *ProductName* item again, and click the up arrow to move it to the top of the *Form Fields* list.

When you reorder the list, the user will see the Product Name field at the top of the page instead of the SKU field, which really is an item for use within the Andes company.

6) Select the *SupplierID* item, change its *Label* to Supplier, choose *Menu* from the *Display As* drop-down menu, and click the *Menu Properties* button.

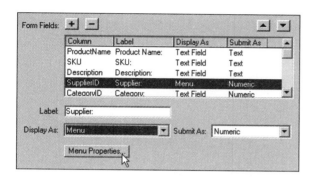

The Menu Properties dialog box opens. This dialog box is where you control whether the menu is populated manually or from a database. This task shows you both methods.

7) Select the *From Database* radio button; then set the *Get Labels From* menu to *CompanyName* and the *Get Values From* menu to *SupplierID*. Click *OK* to close the dialog box.

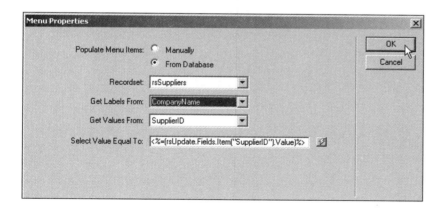

The Insert Record Update Form dialog box reappears. As you know by now, using *CompanyName* for the labels and *SupplierID* for the values lets you apply user-friendly names to the menu, even as the ID number is used behind the scenes.

153

8) Select the *CategoryID* item in the *Form Fields* list, choose *Radio Group* from the *Display As* drop-down menu, and click the *Radio Group Properties* button.

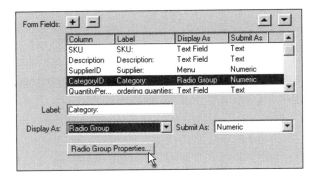

The Radio Group Properties dialog box appears.

9) Select the *From Database* radio button; then set the *Get Labels From* menu to *CategoryName* and the *Get Values From* menu to *CategoryID*. Click *OK* to close the dialog box and return to the Insert Record Update Form dialog box.

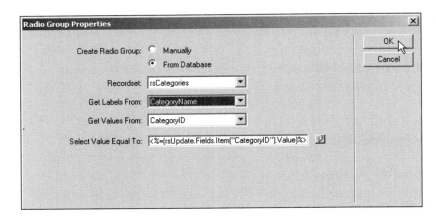

Just as you did with the supplier names in step 7, this step lets you display recognizable category names instead of numbers.

154

10) Select the *DeliveryTime* item in the *Form Fields* list; change its *Label* to `Delivery Time, days:`; and choose *Radio Group* from the *Display As* drop-down menu. Then click the *Radio Group Properties* button.

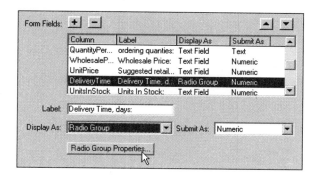

The Radio Group Properties dialog box appears.

11) Select the *Manually* radio button, replace *button1* with 30 in the *Label* text field, and type 30 in the Value text field. Click the + button to create a new label of 15 and a value of 15. Repeat this step to add label-value pairs of 8–8 and 5–5; then click *OK*.

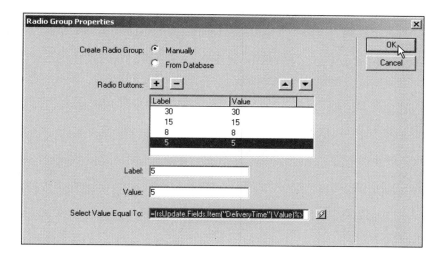

The Insert Record Update Form dialog box reappears, reflecting all the label and display changes you've made.

12) Scroll slowly through the *Form Fields* list, checking your work again.

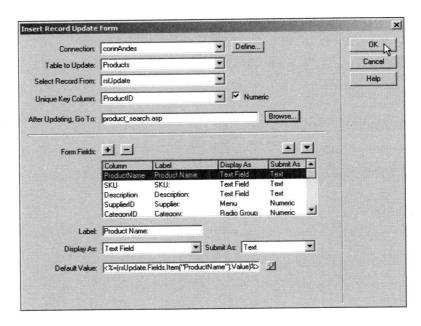

Remember that live-object dialog boxes such as this one cannot be recalled for editing, so be sure your settings are correct before you click *OK* to close the dialog box. After you close the dialog box, UltraDev creates and displays the update page. The server behaviors required to run the page are created automatically.

Click the Preview in Browser button (F12) when the update page appears. The update page opens in your default Web browser.

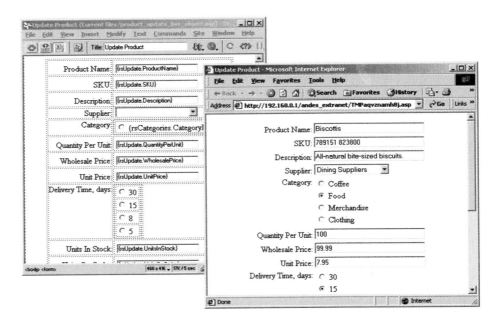

Save the page, click the page's File Management button, and choose Put (Ctrl+Shift+U Windows, Command+Shift+U Macintosh) to move the file to the remote server. Click *Yes* when asked if you want to include dependent files.

ADDING AN UPDATE LINK

Because you did not place an update link in the detail page in Lesson 4, you need to do that before you can start building an update page on a field-by-field basis.

1) Open the product_detail page, scroll to the bottom, click just right of the *Insert* button, and add a couple of nonbreaking spaces (Shift+Ctrl+spacebar in Windows, Shift+Command+spacebar on the Macintosh).

This is the area where you will add a new button.

2) Click the Insert Image icon in the Common Objects palette. Navigate to your local site's *images* folder, and select *frm-update.gif*.

The Update image is added to the page. But you need to add a behavior before the image becomes a button that does anything.

3) With *frm-update.gif* still selected, click the + button in the Server Behaviors panel, and choose *Go To Detail Page* from the drop-down menu.

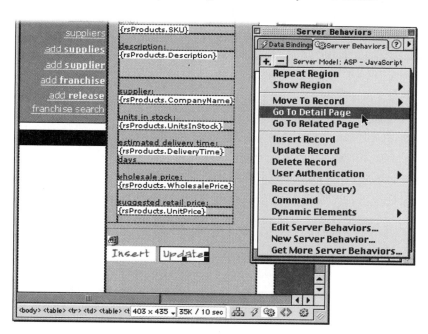

The Go To Detail Page dialog box opens.

4) Change *ProductID* in the *Pass URL Parameter* text window to id**, click *OK*, and save the page.**

Leave the rest of the dialog box's settings as you found them.

This task completes the work needed to link the product_detail page to the product_update page. You may notice that these steps are essentially the same steps you used in "Linking a Results List to a Detail Page" in Lesson 5 . Now you need to complete the work on the product_update page that you started in Lesson 4.

CREATING AN UPDATE PAGE FIELD BY FIELD

As you did in Lesson 6, you'll now build an update page manually. By the way, it's standard to allow access to a product update form directly from a detail page. You could also have a link from the results page, if you wanted, but at the very least, you want to link from the page that displays complete product details. By doing so, you can put all the detail page's text into editable form—at the click of a button.

1) Open the product_update page, click the *Data Bindings* panel, and double-click *Recordset (rsUpdate)*.

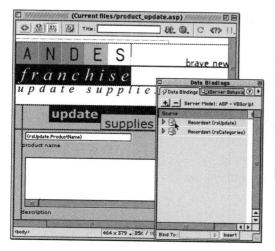
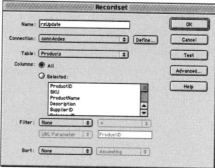

The Recordset dialog box opens. If the dialog box opens with the advanced form displayed, switch to the simple form by clicking the *Simple* button. (If the *Advanced* button is visible, you're already in the simple form.)

2) Use the *Filter* drop-down menu to choose *ProductID*, then replace *ProductID* with id.

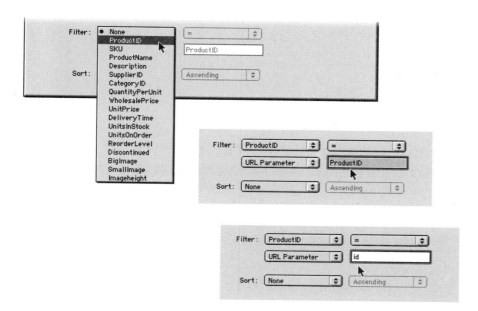

The complete filter statement in the dialog box should read: *ProductID=URL Parameter id.*

159

3) Click the *Test* button in the Recordset dialog box. Enter any number between 1 and 22 in the Test Value text field, and click *OK*.

The test values appear in the Test SQL Statement dialog box.

4) Click *OK* to close the Test dialog box; then click *OK* to close the Recordset dialog box.

Save the product_update page, click the page's File Management button, and choose Put (Ctrl+Shift+U Windows, Command+Shift+U Macintosh) to move the file to the remote server. Click *Yes* when you're asked whether you want to include dependent files. Do the same for the product_detail page.

5) Open the product_resultlist page in your Web browser, and click the detail link for any product.

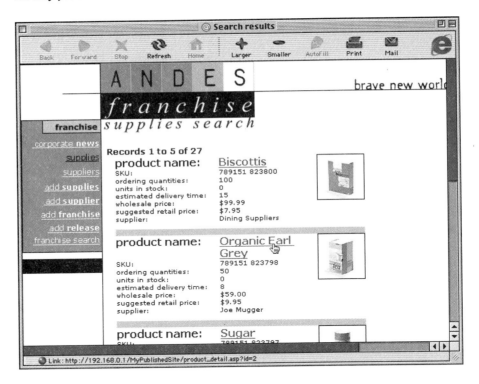

The product_detail page for the selected product appears in your browser.

6) Click the *Update* button at the bottom of the product_detail page.

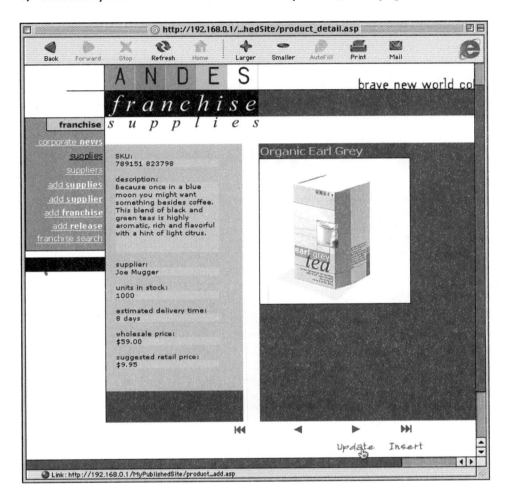

The data from that product's detail page appears in the update_page forms. It's ready for updating after you make the input fields dynamic and apply the update server behavior.

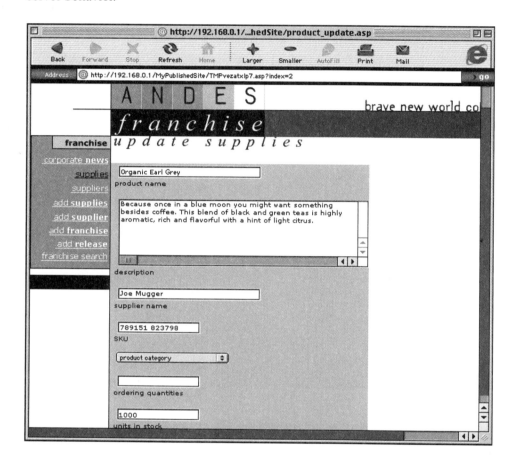

COMPLETING THE INPUT FIELDS

You're in the home stretch now. All that's left to do is reopen the product_update page, complete the input fields, and then apply the actual update behavior to the page. In "Making Form Objects Dynamic" in Lesson 4, you should have inserted a dynamic list element for the product category, a set of radio buttons for the delivery time, and a dynamic checkbox for discontinued products.

1) Reopen the product_update page, delete the text box above *supplier name*, choose *Forms* from the Objects panel's drop-down menu, and click the *Insert List/Menu* icon.

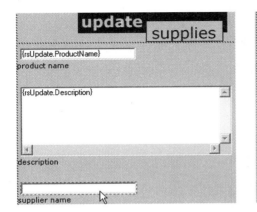 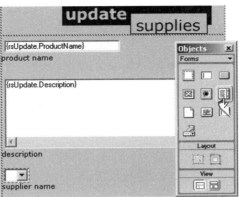

A menu form is inserted just above the *supplier name* label.

2) With the new menu still selected, click the + button in the Server Behaviors panel and choose *Dynamic Elements > Dynamic List/Menu* from the drop-down menu.

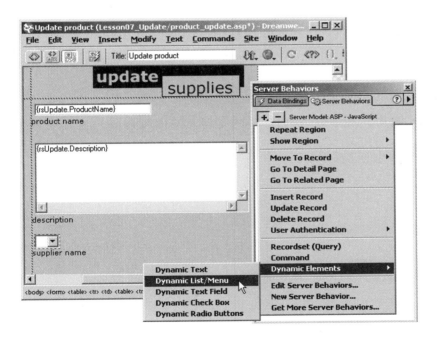

The Dynamic List/Menu dialog box opens.

163

3) Use the drop-down menus to set *Recordset* to *rsSuppliers*, *Get Labels From* to *CompanyName*, and *Get Values From* to *SupplierID*. Click the lightning-bolt icon next to the *Select Value Equal To* text box.

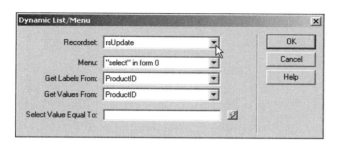

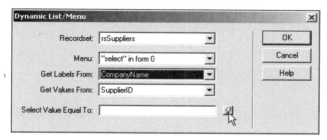

Pay particular attention to the *Recordset* option, because the menu does not show *rsSupplier* automatically. When you click the lightning-bolt icon, the Dynamic Data dialog box appears.

4) Click the *+* next to *Recordset(rsUpdate)* to expand the recordset. Select the *SupplierID* field, and click *OK* to close the Dynamic Data dialog box.

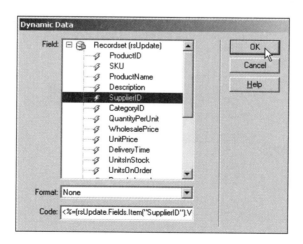

The Dynamic List/Menu dialog box reappears, and the *SupplierID* value has been inserted into the *Select Value Equal To* text window.

164

5) Click _OK_ to close the Dynamic List/Menu dialog box.

Combined with your Lesson 4 work, this task finishes the necessary data-binding work on the product_update page. You have just one task left: applying the update server behavior to the page.

APPLYING THE UPDATE SERVER BEHAVIOR

Now that you've bound all the needed data to the fields in the product_update page, you have to apply the server behavior that makes it possible for you to update the page from within a Web browser.

1) Scroll to the bottom of the product_update page, select the _update_ button, click the + button in the Server Behaviors panel, and choose _Update Record_ from the drop-down menu.

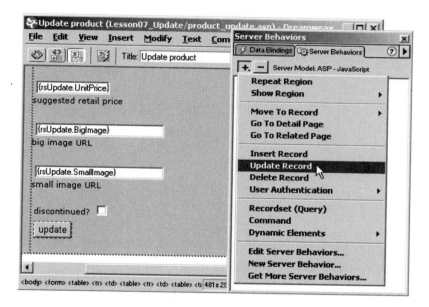

The Update Record dialog box opens.

2) Make sure that *Connection* **is set to** *connAndes*; *Table to Update* **to** *Products*; *Select Record From* **to** *rsUpdate*; *Unique Key Column* **to** *ProductID*; **and** *After Updating, Go To* **to product_search.**

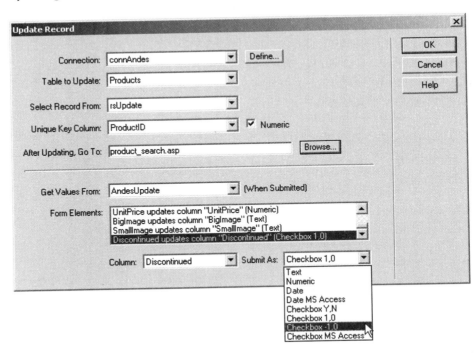

Most of the fields in the top half of the dialog box are set properly. But you'll have to change one field in the *Form Elements* list manually.

3) Scroll to the bottom of the *Form Elements* **list, select the Discontinued item, and use the** *Submit As* **drop-down menu to change the value to** *Checkbox –1,0.*

This is one of the few instances where UltraDev doesn't supply the correct value automatically.

4) Click *OK* **to close the dialog box.**

Save the page, click the page's File Management button, and choose Put (Ctrl+ Shift+U Windows, Command+Shift+U Macintosh) to move the file to the remote server. Click *Yes* when you are asked whether you want to include dependent files.

5) Open the product_resultlist page in your Web browser, and click the link for Organic Earl Grey tea to see its detail page.

The detail page for Organic Earl Grey tea appears in your browser.

6) Click the *update* button at the bottom of the product_detail page.

Your browser displays the product_update page, with all the previous product's details appearing in forms that have editable fields.

7) Change *blue moon* to red moon in the tea's description field in the product_update page, and click the *update* button again.

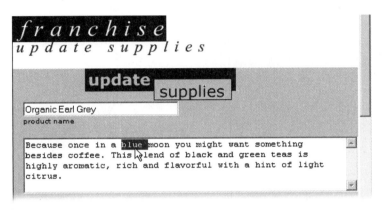

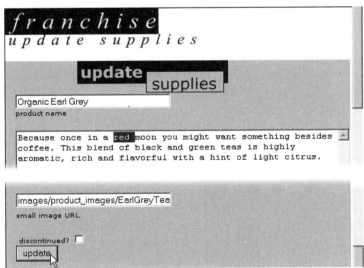

Nothing appears to happen; in fact, the product_update page looks just the same. But big changes have occurred, as you'll see when you browse back to the detail page for the product you just changed.

8) Browse to the detail page for the Organic Earl Grey tea, the product you just changed.

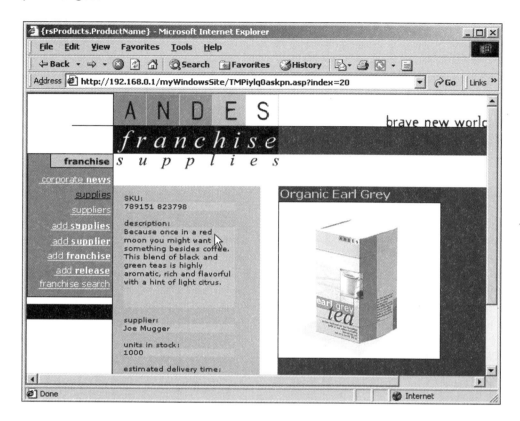

As you can see, the changes you made in step 7 (replacing *blue* with *red*)) now appear in the product_detail page.

In the next lesson, you will add more menu elements to the product_search page. By binding those menu elements to SQL variables, you can create increasingly precise searches.

WHAT YOU HAVE LEARNED

In this lesson you have:

- Used UltraDev's Record Update Form live object to create an update page that lets users change database records via a Web browser (pages 150–157)

- Created an update page that can pull data from any product detail page into forms with editable fields (page 158–162)

- Created dynamic menus that let you find, quickly and by supplier, the products you want to update (pages 162–165)

- Applied the update server behavior, which enables you to update the appropriate database record from within your Web browser (pages 165–168)

creating searches with sql variables

LESSON 8

Pages you provide for users to search a database can be as simple or as complicated as you like. You probably have your own favorite search pages that you use as you surf the Web. What all search pages have in common is one or more form elements in which the search criteria can be set as well as a Submit button to start the search. In this lesson, you will use dynamic menu elements to create simple—and more complex—searches.

In this lesson, you'll learn how to create multiple-category search pages with sophisticated wild-card options.

Every UltraDev recordset is built with a database query statement, which defines the criteria that find and extract data from the database. UltraDev uses Structured Query Language, or SQL (pronounced sequel), to create your queries. As you've already seen, you don't need to understand SQL to build simple recordsets. If you do understand SQL, however, UltraDev can use it to define and filter your recordset with a great deal of precision.

WHAT YOU WILL LEARN

In this lesson, you will:

- Build a simple search page
- Define SQL variables for a search page
- Create a multiple category search page
- Add flexibility and power to a search page by allowing wild-card searches

APPROXIMATE TIME

It usually takes about one hour to complete this lesson.

LESSON FILES

Media Files:

None

Starting Files:

*UltraDev 4 Lessons\…\Current
files\product_search*

*UltraDev 4 Lessons\…\Current
files\product_resultlist*

Completed Project:

Same as Starting Files

BUILDING A SIMPLE SEARCH PAGE

Before you learn how to create more sophisticated search pages, you'll want to create a basic search page.

1) Open the product_search page, and copy the *rsCategories* recordset into the Data Bindings panel.

Use the right-click (Windows) or Control-click (Macintosh) trick to copy the recordset from the product_update page and then paste it into the product_search page.

2) Click the page's *<form>* tag in the tag selector, and when the property inspector opens, type `ProductSearch` **in the *Form Name* text field. Click the folder button next to the *Action* text field, and browse to your site's product_resultlist page. Set the Method drop-down menu to *GET*.**

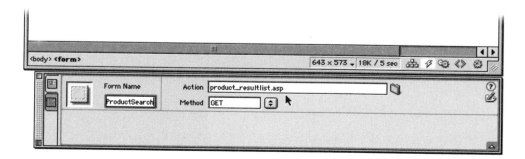

172

These settings point the search page's action to the product_resultlist page. That way, Web users who click the page's *search* button will be sent to the results page, where the found items will be displayed.

3) Click the search page's *product category* menu to select it, and type Category **in the property inspector's *List/Menu* text field. With the *product category* menu still selected, click the + button in the Server Behaviors panel, and choose *Dynamic Elements > Dynamic List/Menu* from the drop-down menu.**

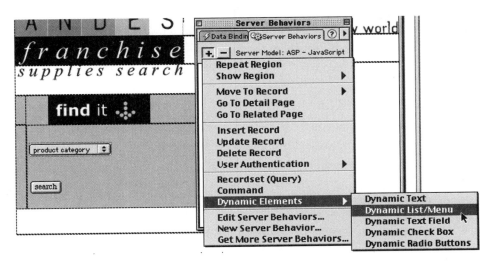

The Dynamic List/Menu dialog box opens.

4) Using the drop-down menus, set *Recordset* to *rsCategories*, *Get Labels From* to *CategoryName*, and *Get Values From* to *CategoryID*. Then click *OK* to close the dialog box.

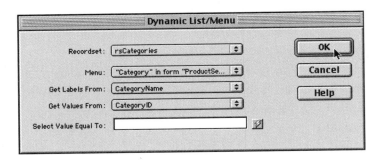

The *Menu* option is set automatically. Leave the *Select Value Equal To* text field blank.

Here's what's going on in the dialog box: Instead of using a server behavior to transfer search criteria to the results page, you're going to submit the ProductSearch form to that page and then filter the results with a request object, which you'll create in the next task. By the way, in ASP and JSP, the request object by definition holds name-value pairs representing form data submitted from the preceding page. ColdFusion calls this a form object, but the same logic applies.

5) Save the page, click the page's File Management button, and choose Put (Ctrl+ Shift+U Windows, Command+Shift+U Macintosh) to move the file to the remote server. Click *Yes* when you are asked whether you want to include dependent files.

That's all you need to do to this page for the moment. The next task involves using a request object to filter the recordset.

DEFINING SQL VARIABLES

To retrieve a searched value, you must use the correct expression for your server type (see the note in this section). In this task, where you'll be using the GET method from the preceding task, you would retrieve the CategoryName value as Request.QueryString("Category") for the ASP server model, request.getParameter("Category") for JSP, or URL.Category for ColdFusion.

The string which this expression evaluates will be used to filter the recordset that displays products on the results page. But you cannot use a query directly in a typical SQL WHERE clause, such as this:

```
WHERE CategoryName = Request.QueryString("Category")
```

Instead, you need to define a so-called SQL variable—call it CAT—and make sure that CAT takes on the appropriate value when the request is made. UltraDev's advanced Recordset dialog box contains options that make this process as simple as possible.

NOTE *When a form is submitted, the array of submitted data is available for server-side scripting on the receiving page in a request, form, or URL object, depending on the server technology and the form method. If the form's method is* GET, *the request syntax is ASP:* Request.QueryString(); *JSP:* request.getParameter(); *or ColdFusion:* URL.[variable]. *If the method is* POST, *the syntax is ASP:* Request.Form(); *JSP:* request.getParameter(); *or ColdFusion:* Form.[variable].

1) Open the product_resultlist page, and double-click *Recordset (rsProducts)* in the Data Bindings panel.

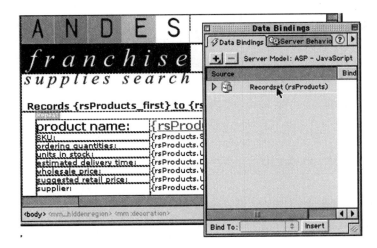

The Recordset dialog box opens in its advanced form. (If the *Simple* button is visible, you're already in the advanced form.)

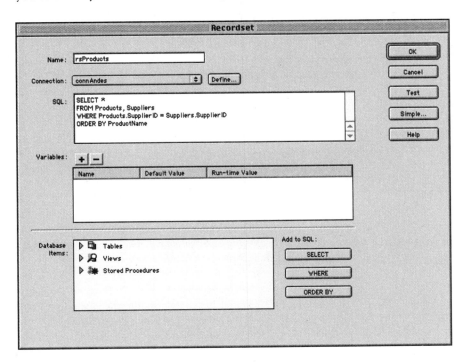

2) To filter by the CategoryName field, include that field in the query by typing directly in the *SQL* window. As you type, compare the original statement in the preceding figure above with the following statement (be sure to delete *ORDER BY ProductName* in the SQL window):

```
SELECT *
FROM Products, Suppliers, Categories
WHERE Products.SupplierID=Suppliers.SupplierID
AND Products.CategoryID=Categories.CategoryID
```

When you're done, the dialog box should look like the following figure.

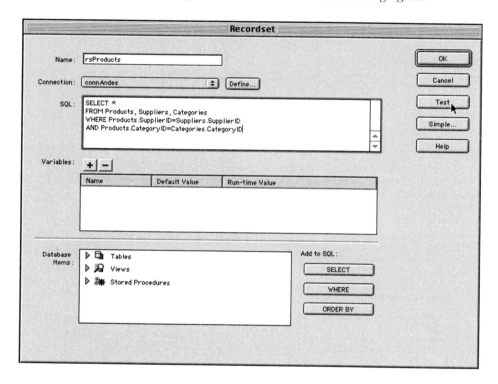

TIP *By copying and pasting parts of the opening SQL statement, you can save yourself a lot of keyboarding—and reduce the likelihood of a typo.*

3) Click the *Test* button.

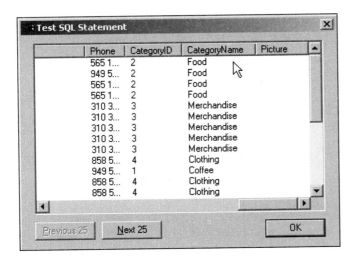

The Test SQL Statement dialog box appears, displaying a *CategoryName* column along with a *CategoryID* column. (You'll need to scroll way to the right to see it.) Click OK to close the dialog box.

4) In the Recordset dialog box, click the *Variables +* button. In the text field, type CAT as the *Name*, Food as the *Default Value*, and Request.QueryString ("Category") as the Run-time Value.

Although this example uses the ASP syntax, remember to substitute the JSP or ColdFusion syntax if you're using one of those server models. By the way, Food is a temporary setting for Default Value that allows you to test the statement.

5) Type a new line into the SQL window: AND CategoryName='CAT' at the bottom of the SQL window.

177

The Recordset dialog box should now look like the following figure.

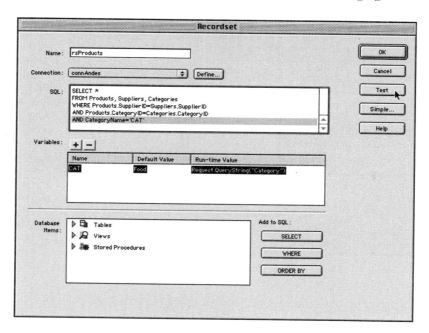

6) Click the *Test* button again.

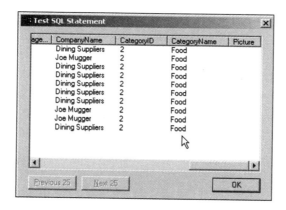

The Test SQL Statement dialog box displays only products in the Food category. (Again, if you want to see this for yourself, you'll have to scroll to the right.) Click *OK* to close the dialog box.

7) Save the page, click the page's File Management button, and choose Put (Ctrl+ Shift+U Windows, Command+Shift+U Macintosh) to move the file to the remote server. Click *Yes* when you are asked whether you want to include dependent files. When you finish this step, close the page.

8) Open the product_search page in your Web browser, choose a product category from the drop-down menu, and click the *search* button.

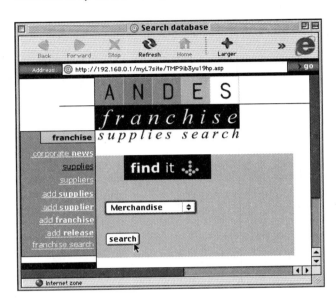

Your browser switches to the product_resultlist page and displays only the products in the selected category.

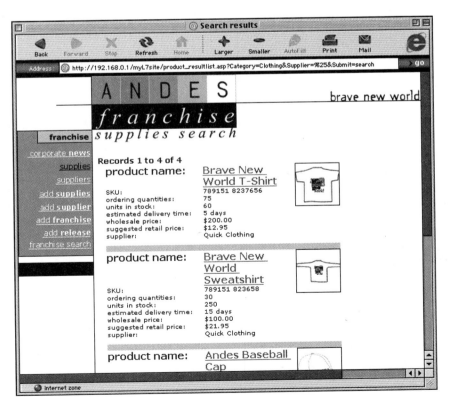

179

The simple version of the Recordset dialog box would be perfectly capable of handling this search task—in fact, the search would be much easier to do in that dialog box. After all, the simple dialog box has pop-up menus for managing record filtering; creates a SQL variable behind the scenes; and offers the usual mathematical and string operators (such as begins with and includes) for record filtering. But the simple dialog box could not be used in this exercise, because the recordset on the product_resultlist page joins data from two data tables.

In the next task, you will need a second SQL variable, and that task also requires that you use the advanced version of the Recordset dialog box.

ADDING A SECOND SEARCH CRITERION

Search pages are often called on to do double duty, particularly when the database is large and a single search criterion would yield an unacceptably large amount of data. Filtering the General Motors personnel database for shop-floor workers, for example, would yield thousands of names. A search for shop floor workers who were hired in 1999 would be far more manageable.

The Andes Coffee database is not exactly General Motors, but a double search is a useful exercise nevertheless. In the following task, you are going to create a search by product category and by supplier.

1) Reopen the product_search page, and copy the *rsSuppliers* recordset into the Data Bindings panel.

Use the right-click (Windows) or Control-click (Macintosh) trick to copy the rsSuppliers recordset from the product_add page and then paste it into the product_search page.

2) Click in the product_search page just after the *category* menu, add some space, and type supplier.

3) Choose *Forms* from the Objects panel's drop-down menu; then click the *Insert List/Menu* button to add a second menu next to the supplier label. With the menu selected, type `Supplier` in the *List/Menu* text field of the property inspector.

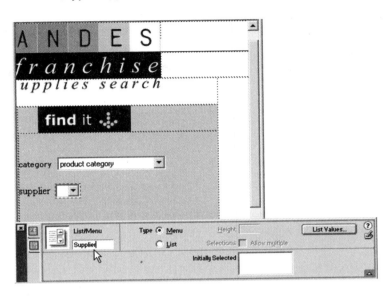

4) With the menu still selected, click the **+** button in the Server Behaviors panel and choose Dynamic Elements > Dynamic List/Menu from the drop-down menu.

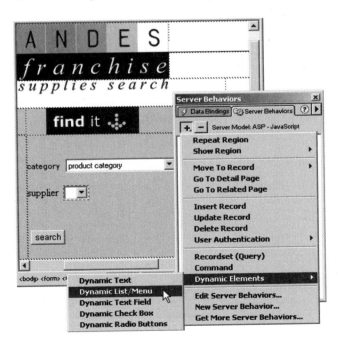

The Dynamic List/Menu dialog box opens.

5) Use the drop-down menus to set *Recordset* to *rsSuppliers*, *Get Labels From* to *CompanyName*, and *Get Values From* to *CompanyName*. Click *OK* to close the dialog box and save the page.

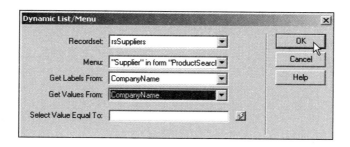

The *Menu* option is set automatically. Leave the *Select Value Equal To* text field blank.

As you probably realize, this setup is the same one you created when building the simple search page. The difference comes in the next task.

IMPLEMENTING A TWO-DIMENSIONAL SEARCH

In the preceding task, you added a second search criterion, but before you can perform a two-dimensional search, you need to add both variables to your query. As always, you make those additions in the Recordset dialog box.

1) Open the product_resultlist page, and double-click the rsProducts recordset.

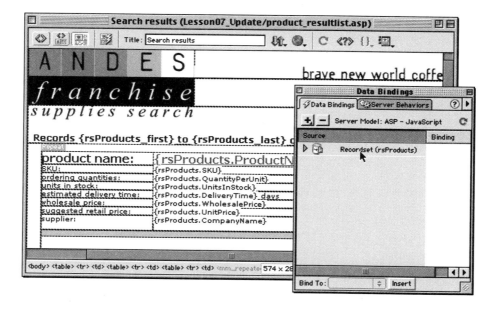

The recordset's dialog box will open in the advanced form.

2) Click the *Variables +* button. In the text field, type SUP **as the *Name*,** Dining
Supplies **as the *Default Value*, and** Request.QueryString("Supplier") **as the**
Run-time Value.

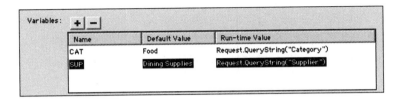

Remember to substitute the JSP or ColdFusion syntax if you're using one of those
server models.

3) Type AND CompanyName='SUP' **at the bottom of the SQL window.**
The Recordset dialog box should now look like the following figure.

4) Click the *Test* button.

The Test SQL Statement dialog box appears, displaying only food products from the Dining Supplies company. (To see for yourself, you'll have to scroll to the far right.) Click *OK* to close the dialog box.

5) Save the product_resultlist page; then move it and the product_search page to the remote server. Click *Yes* when you are asked whether you want to include dependent files.

When you finish this step, close both pages.

6) Open the product_search page in your Web browser, use the *category* and *supplier* menus to create a combination search, and click the *search* button.

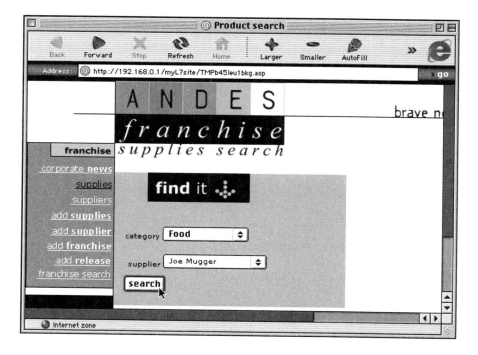

Your browser switches to the product_resultlist page and display only the products that meet both search criteria.

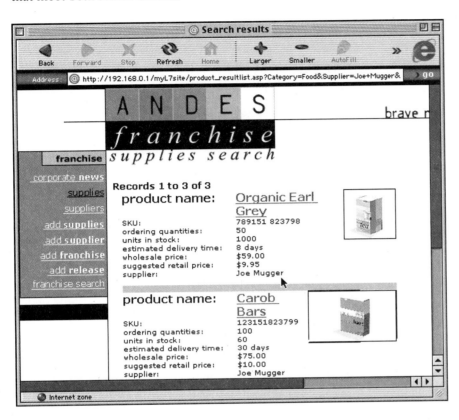

ALLOWING WILD CARDS IN SEARCHES

The main drawback of two-dimensional searching is that users must use both dimensions in building their searches. As the search page now stands, users have no way of searching for food from any supplier or any product from Dining Suppliers, for example. You have to use both criteria—unless you allow wild cards to be used in such searches.

1) Reopen the product_resultlist page, and double-click the rsProducts recordset.

The Recordset dialog box opens in advanced form.

2) In the Variables list, type % in the Default Value column for both *CAT* and *SUP*, replacing *Food* and *Dining Supplies*.

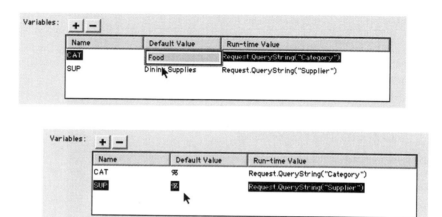

The percent sign (%) will be interpreted as "any string," much like the asterisk (*) works in the SQL statement "SELECT * ". You need to make a small edit in the SQL statement before this wild-card character will be allowed, however.

3) Change the last two lines that you typed in the SQL window, replacing the equal sign (=) by typing LIKE. The first of those lines should now read *AND CategoryName LIKE 'CAT'*. The second of those lines should read *AND CompanyName LIKE 'SUP'*.

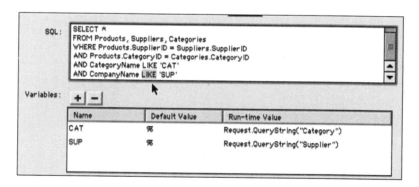

The SQL operator LIKE ensures that only values equal to CAT will be returned. But because you redefined CAT with the wild-card character % in the *Variables* list, you're essentially telling UltraDev that it can use any *CategoryName* or *CompanyName* in the search. Click the Test button, and you'll get exactly those results.

4) Save the page and close it.

186

ADDING STATIC OPTIONS TO SEARCHES

You have not yet changed the functioning of the search. You've just shown that wild cards will work as long as the SQL syntax is correct. To make such searches possible in the actual Andes Coffee pages, you need to find some way to enable the user to pass the percent sign (%) as data. That's where static options come in.

1) Reopen the product_search page, and click the *category* menu to select it. Open the property inspector (Ctrl+F3 Windows, Command+F3 Mac), and click the *List Values* button.

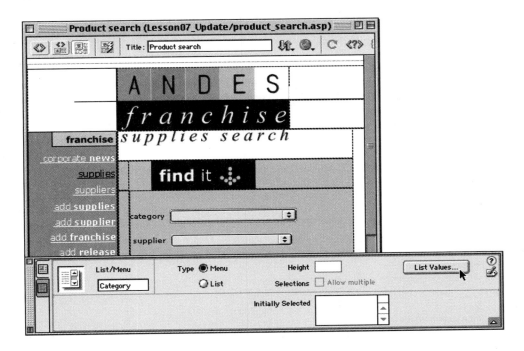

The List Values dialog box opens, listing a single server expression.

2) Click the + button, and type Any category **in the *Item Label* column and** % **in the *Value* column.**

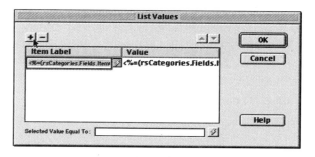

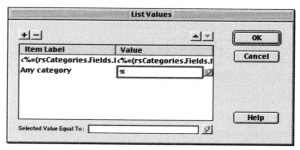

3) Press Enter (Windows) or Return (Mac); then click the up arrow to move the new list value to the top of the list.

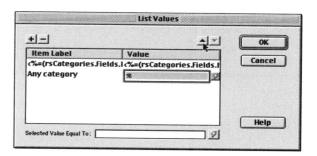

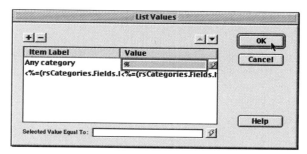

This step allows the % value to be passed as data in any category.

4) Repeat steps 1 through 3 for the product_search page's supplier menu, typing Any supplier **as the Item Label and** % **as the Value.**

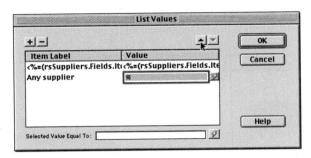

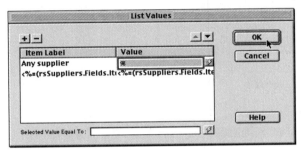

This task—combined with allowing wild cards—makes it possible for users to perform a two-dimensional search without having to fill in both criteria.

5) Save the product_search page; then move it and the product_resultlist page to the remote server. Click *Yes* when you are asked whether you want to include dependent files.

When you finish this step, close both pages.

189

6) Open the product_search page in your Web browser, set the *category menu* to *Any category* and the *supplier menu* to *Joe Mugger*, and click the *search* button.

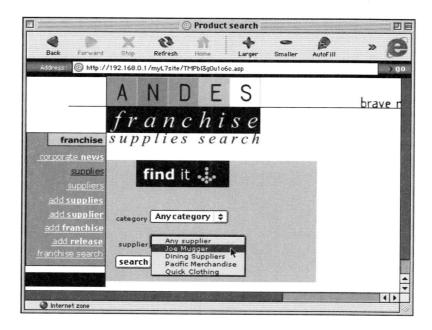

Your browser switches to the product_resultlist page and displays all products supplied by Joe Mugger.

Based on this lesson, you should be able to build a search page that offers users multiple ways to search a database. In Lesson 9, you'll see how to use server objects to pass information across a site's pages.

WHAT YOU HAVE LEARNED

In this lesson, you have:

- Built a simple search page by using form elements and populated them with dynamic data pulled from the Andes Coffee database (pages 172–174)
- Used the advanced form of the Recordset dialog box to define SQL variables for your searches (pages 174–180)
- Added search criteria to enable two-dimensional searching (pages 180–185)
- Made it possible to use wild-card characters in searches so that users are not forced to use every criterion when creating a search query (pages 185–190)

displaying server objects

The whole point of server technologies such as ASP, JSP, and ColdFusion is to enable a Web server to do more than the basic HTTP protocol allows. You have seen plenty of examples already: database connectivity, dynamic page elements, navigation with recordsets, and data records filtered by user-supplied criteria. You've built all of these server-side capabilities into your pages using the Data Bindings and Server Behaviors panel, without necessarily being aware of the source code that was created for your pages. By understanding a bit of the behind-the-scenes code, however, you can extend UltraDev's potential.

By using a request object, you can create a handy reminder inside the product search page that tells users what criteria they used for their search (in this case, Coffee from any supplier).

All three server models include a set of objects that you can use to pass information across pages. The objects are always available on any page at your site, but to use them, you need to add them to the Data Bindings panel, just as you do for recordsets. The principal server objects are the request object (which ColdFusion splits into a URL object and a form object), the response object, and the session object.

The most common type of request object holds data passed from page to page by submitting a form or by passing a special URL parameter (as you did in Lesson 8). The response object passes data from the server, either outputting page text or redirecting the user to another URL. The session object, a unique nonpersistent cookie, holds anything you choose to put there and lasts the length of a user's session. Cookies are covered in more depth in Lesson 10.

NOTE *To use the session object in Cold Fusion, you need to have a text file called application.cfm in the server directory where your site files reside. The file includes this text:*
CFAPPLICATION NAME="application name" SESSIONMANAGEMENT="Yes">

WHAT YOU WILL LEARN

In this lesson, you will:

- Use a request object to retrieve data from one page
- Pass that data to another page by using the Data Bindings panel's Request Variable behavior
- Substitute user-friendly text automatically whenever code-based static option symbols might appear on the results page

APPROXIMATE TIME

It usually takes about one hour to complete this lesson.

LESSON FILES

Media Files:

None

Starting Files:

UltraDev 4 Lessons\...\Current files\product_resultlist

UltraDev 4 Lessons\...\Current files\product_search

Completed Project:

Same as Starting Files

USING A REQUEST OBJECT TO RETRIEVE DATA

You're going to use a request, or form, object to remind users of the search criteria they originally entered in the product_search page. You'll be using the request form you built in Lesson 8 for the product_search and product_resultlist pages. The product_search page used two GET forms (one for category and one for supplier) to filter the search results displayed in the product_resultlist page. This task will enable search criteria used in the product_search page to be passed to the product_resultlist page.

1) Open the product_resultlist page, click the + button in the Data Bindings panel, and choose *Request Variable* from the drop-down menu.

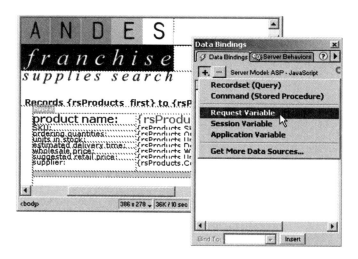

The Request Variable dialog box opens. If you're using ColdFusion, choose *URL* from the Data Bindings panel's drop-down menu to open the URL Variable dialog box.

2) If you're using ASP, choose *Request QueryString* from the *Type* drop-down menu.

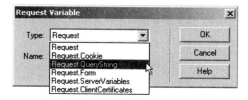

If you're using JSP or ColdFusion, your choices will reflect that server technology's syntax (see "Defining SQL Variables" in Lesson 8). In this case, the JSP choice would be *getParameter*, and the ColdFusion choice would be *Variable*.

In ASP, simply leaving the Type menu set to Request would work fine, but choosing Request QueryString will be easier to work with in this exercise.

3) Type Category **in the *Name* text field, and click *OK* to close the dialog box.**

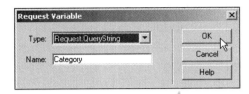

4) Repeat steps 1 through 3, typing Supplier **in the *Name* text field. Then click *OK* to close the dialog box.**

5) Click the product_resultlist page just below the franchise supplies search headline, insert a carriage return to give yourself some space, and type Result of search for from.

Although the phrase *Result of search for from* doesn't make much sense by itself, you'll see its purpose when you complete this task.

6) Open the CSS Styles panel (Shift+F11), select the *Result of search for from* line, and apply the *newlist* style to it.

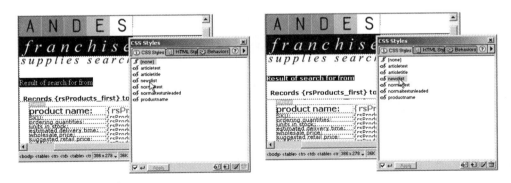

The style of the line now matches that of the Records 1 to 5 of 7 that you first created in Lesson 5.

7) Expand the *Request* item in the Data Bindings panel, select the *Category* variable, and drag it onto the page between the words *for* and *from*.

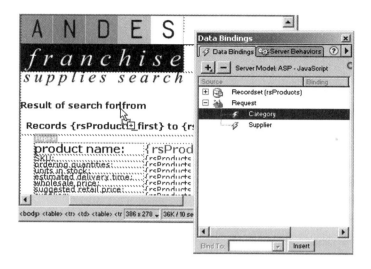

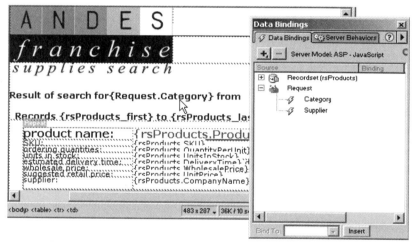

A placeholder for the Request.Category variable is inserted into the line. You may need to go back and add a character space before or after the placeholder to ensure that the line reads clearly. It can be hard to tell how the actual data will look until you switch to the Live Data view or look at the page in your Web browser.

8) In the Data Bindings panel, select the *Supplier* variable, and drag it onto the page after the word *from*.

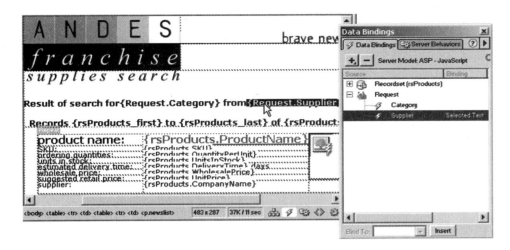

Take a look at what you've changed so far by selecting the Category placeholder, clicking the Show Code and Design View button, and inspecting the code you've added.

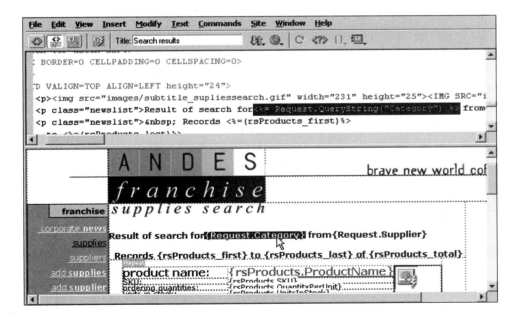

If you're using ASP, you should see this:

```
<%= Request.QueryString ("Category")%>
```

In JSP, you should see this:

```
<%=((request.getParameter("category")!=null)?request.getParameter("category"
):"") %>
```

And in ColdFusion, you should see this:

```
<cfoutput>#URL.category#</cfoutput>
```

Before you can use these new variables, you'll need to make a few changes in Live Data view. In the next task, you'll see how Live Data view helps you gauge more accurately what values will be used.

DEFINING REQUEST VARIABLES AS DATA SOURCES

In this task, you'll make it possible for the request variable to appear on the page by specifying a query string that will be passed to the results page. As you'll discover at the end of this task, however, what you see in Live Data view and what you get in browse view may not always be the same.

1) With the product_resultlist page still open, switch to Live Data view by clicking its button in the toolbar or choosing View > Live Data (Ctrl+Shift+R Windows, Command+Shift+R Mac).

The page's placeholders disappear, leaving the unfinished text *Result of search for from.*

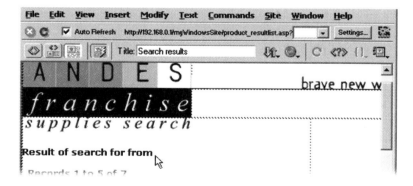

2) Click the *Settings* button in the Live Data View toolbar.

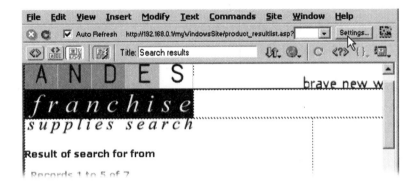

The Live Data Settings dialog box appears.

3) Click the *URL Request* + button, type Category **in the *Name* column and** Food **in the Value column. Click the + button again, and type** Supplier **in the second Name column and** Dining Suppliers **in the second *Value* column.**

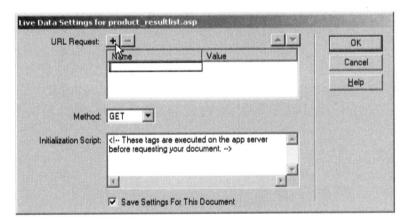

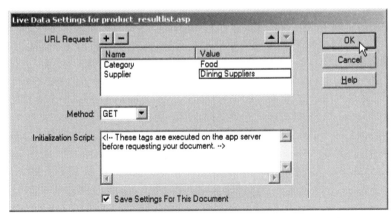

Leave the *Method* drop-down menu set to *GET*, ignore the text in the *Initialization Script* list, and click *OK* to close the dialog box. These changes will ensure that the placeholders in the *Result of search for from* text display actual values, as you'll see if you click the Refresh button.

4) Test the request variables by opening the product_search page in your Web browser, choosing various combinations from the *category* and *supplier* drop-down menus, and clicking the *search* button.

In most cases, the search results display correctly in your Web browser. You'll find there's a snag, however, whenever you choose *Any category* from the *category* menu or *Any supplier* from the *supplier* menu.

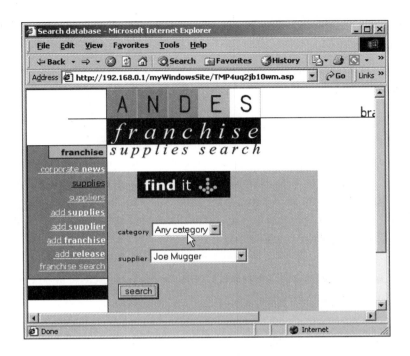

Instead of displaying the words *Any category* or *Any supplier* in the product_resultlist page's search-criteria line, your browser displays a percent sign (%).

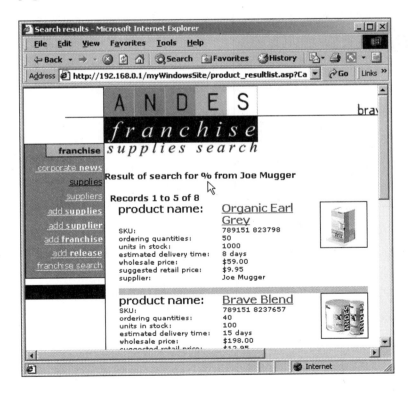

This situation occurs because the actual data being sent by the request is not *Any category* or *Any supplier* but %, which was the static option you created at the end of Lesson 8. This isn't good, because the whole of point of adding the search-criteria line is to make things clearer for users. Fixing this problem is the focus of the next task.

DISPLAYING SYMBOL ALTERNATIVES FOR STATIC OPTIONS

Fixing the problem of the percent sign (%) showing up instead of a user-friendly term is relatively easy, but it requires some hand coding—something you normally don't have to do much in UltraDev. Rest assured; the process is fairly straightforward as long as you pay attention to balancing your tags by pairing every single opening parenthesis, bracket, and brace with a closing one.

1) With the product_resultlist page still open and Live Data view still active, select the word *Food* and switch to Code view.

The Code view opens. In ASP, the Food request variable appears as:

```
<%= Request.QueryString ("Category")%>
```

In JSP, you should see this:

```
<%=((request.getParameter("category")!=null)?request.getParameter("category"
):"") %>
```

And in ColdFusion, you should see this:

```
<cfoutput>#URL.category#</cfoutput>
```

TIP *Be sure to click the Code view button rather than the combination Code and Design view button. The combination button creates two views that must be refreshed simultaneously after you change the code—a procedure that UltraDev can have trouble handling.*

2) Type directly in the window to change the highlighted code, based on the server technology you are using.

In ASP/JavaScript, the new code should read as follows:

```
<%if (Request.QueryString ("Category") == "%"){
Response.Write("any product");
}
else {Response.Write(Request.QueryString("Category"))
}
%>
```

In ASP/VBScript, the new code should read as follows:

```
<%If Request.QueryString ("Category") = "%" Then
Response.Write("any product")
Else Response.Write(Request.QueryString("Category"))
End If
%>
```

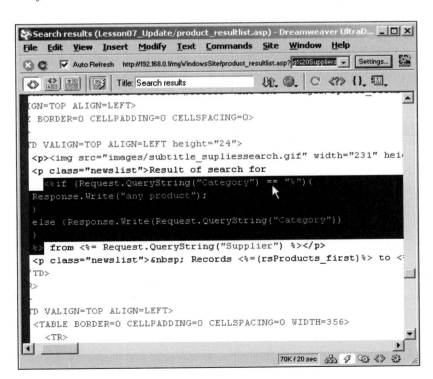

203

In JSP, the new code should read as follows:

```
<%=(((request.getParameter("category")!=null)&& (request.getParameter
("category") != "%")) ?request.getParameter("category"):"any product")%>
```

And in ColdFusion, the new code should read this way:

```
<cfif URL.category EQ "%"><cfoutput>any product</cfoutput>
<cfelse><cfoutput>#URL.category#</cfoutput>
</cfif>
```

Despite the length of the changes, all this code does is have the server check whether the category value is % and, when it is, replaces it with the words "any category." If you're using ASP/JavaScript, be sure to use two equal signs (==) as the comparison operator.

3) Switch to Live Data view, select the word *Supplier*, and then switch back to Code view.

The Code view opens. In ASP, the Supplier request variable is highlighted.

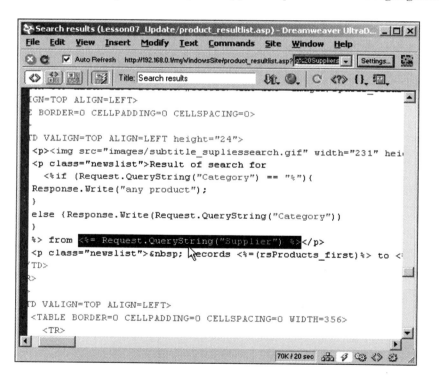

4) Make the same code changes that you did in step 2, but type `supplier` **instead of** *category*.

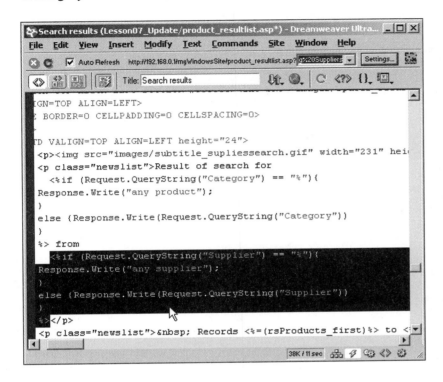

Again, adjust the code based on the server technology you are using. The preceding figure shows the coding for ASP/JavaScript.

5) Save the product_resultlist page, click the page's File Management button, and choose Put (Ctrl+Shift+U Windows, Command+Shift+U Macintosh) to move the file to the remote server. Click *Yes* when you are asked whether you want to include dependent files.

Repeat this step for the product_search page.

6) Test the fix of the % static options by opening the product_search page in your Web browser, choosing *Any category* from the *category* menu and *Any supplier* from the *supplier* menu, and then clicking the *search* button.

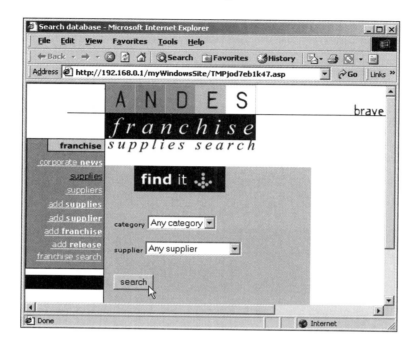

When the product_resultlist page appears in your browser, the percent sign (%) will be replaced by *any category* and *any supplier*. This setup will be much clearer to users.

In the next lesson, you'll learn how to set up security for your site by using passwords and various server behaviors.

WHAT YOU HAVE LEARNED

In this lesson, you have:

- Used a request object to create a line in the product_search page that reminds users what criteria they entered in the search page (pages 194–198)

- Enabled the display of request variables on a Web page by defining them in the Data Bindings panel (pages 198–202)

- Added code so that user-recognizable labels appear in the product_results page instead of the percent sign (%) originally generated by the page's static options (pages 202–206)

setting passwords and security

Here's the fundamental problem of site security: You need to give your site's users enough access to meet their needs but not so much access that they can accidentally, or deliberately, interfere with the site's operation. In particular, pages that control your database (such as the product_add and product_update pages) should be off limits to most users. UltraDev helps you apply a moderate degree of security to your Web sites with four authentication server behaviors; Log In User, Restrict Access to Page, Check New Username, and Log Out User. You'll use the first three behaviors in this lesson. The fourth, Log Out User, simply purges the session object at logout. While such purges are a wise precaution, they're not absolutely necessary, so feel free to explore its use on your own.

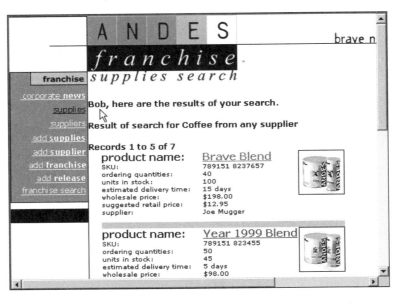

It's easy to create personalized pages for your Web site's users with UltraDev's User Authentication server behaviors.

WHAT YOU WILL LEARN

In this lesson, you will:

- Create a login procedure for existing site users
- Restrict access to certain pages based on the user's group access level
- Personalize pages for users based on their user profiles
- Enable UltraDev to check for duplicate logins

APPROXIMATE TIME

It usually takes about an hour to complete this lesson.

LESSON FILES

Media Files:

none

Starting Files:

UltraDev 4 Lessons\…\Current files\andes_login

UltraDev 4 Lessons\…\Current files\product_search

UltraDev 4 Lessons\…\Current files\andes_login_fail

UltraDev 4 Lessons\…\Current files\product_update

UltraDev 4 Lessons\…\Current files\andes_admin_only

UltraDev 4 Lessons\…\Current files\product_add

UltraDev 4 Lessons\…\Current files\product_detail

UltraDev 4 Lessons\…\Current files\andes_access_denied

UltraDev 4 Lessons\…\Current files\product_resultlist

UltraDev 4 Lessons\…\Current files\andes_newuser

UltraDev 4 Lessons\…\Current files\username_exists

Completed Project:

Same as Starting Files

CREATING LOGINS FOR EXISTING USERS

The main principle behind authentication is that every site user is assigned an access level, which determines the pages the user may see. Access levels are stored in a field in a customer's data table and retrieved at login by matching the user name and password combination that the user supplies. The access level is then stored as a session variable that is readable on any page for the duration of the user's visit to your site.

The Andes Coffee database has a sample Customers data table, which includes fields for the user name, password, access level, real name, address, and so on. You don't have to create access restrictions using such a table, of course, but the example in this task includes three possible access levels: admin, which provides unrestricted access; user, which blocks access to database administration pages and features; and foreign, which is for guests who live overseas and cannot use the site's e-commerce features because of U.S. restrictions on the export of encryption technologies.

1) Open the andes_login page, click the + button in either the Data Bindings or Server Behaviors panel, and choose *Recordset(Query)* from the drop-down menu.

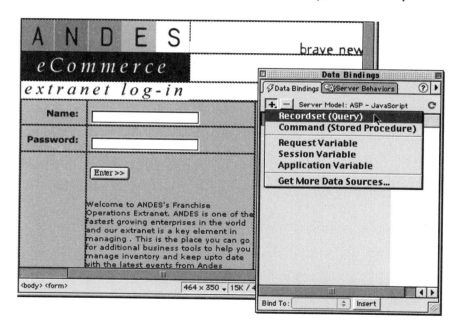

The Recordset dialog box will open. The simple version of the Recordset dialog box should be visible, but if it's not just click the *Simple* button.

2) Name the new recordset rsCustomers, **choose** *connAndes* **as the** *Connection* **and** *Customers* **as the** *Table*. **Choose the** *Selected* **radio button and select these fields from the list:** *CustomerID*, *LastName*, *FirstName*, *Usergroup*, *Username*, **and** *Password*.

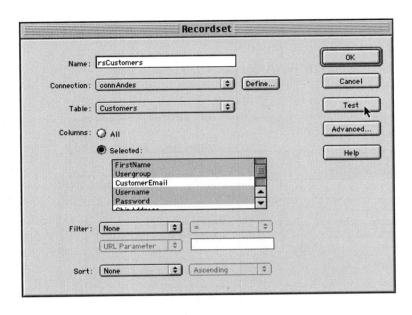

TIP *To select multiple, non-contiguous fields in the list, Ctrl+click (Windows) or Command+click (Mac).*

3) Click *Test*.

d	CustomerID	LastName	FirstName	Usergroup	Username	Password
	54494	Roberts	Bob	admin	bobrob	cheese
	54495	Kim	Lee	admin	ldkim	drums
	54496	Stevenson	Jane	admin	jane	potato
	54497	Freely	Maureen	user	jbates	pumpkin
	54498	Morley	David	user	claus	candy
	54499	Hendrie	Bob	user	blackbart	boo
	54500	Knottenbelt	Elizabeth	admin	howdy	whattimeisit
	54501	Macdonald	Jill	user	mickey	minnie
	54502	Polezzi	Lauredana	user	zac	zac
	54503	Schimmelpennick	Sander	user	jobaby	bluesclues
	54504	Lamb	Mary	user	mary	baa
	54505	van der Weel	Adriaan	user	joe	blow
	54506	Zangmo	Yeshe	user	kako	crow
	54507	Bouvier	Jean–Claude	foreign	bouquet	archives
	54508	Petigree	Charmian	admin	petty	officer
	54509	Tynan	Tex	user	minou	lechat

211

The Test SQL Statement dialog box will appear. Jot down at least one *Username* listing and its companion *Password* that also has a *Usergroup* level of *admin* (such as *bobrob* and *cheese*). Also note the *Username–Password* pair *jbates* and *pumpkin*, which is the first pair in the list whose *Usergroup* is *user*. That pair will be used in the task that follows the current task. Click *OK* to close the dialog box, then click *OK* again to close the recordset dialog box.

4) Click the + button in the Server Behaviors panel and choose *User Authentication > Log In User*.

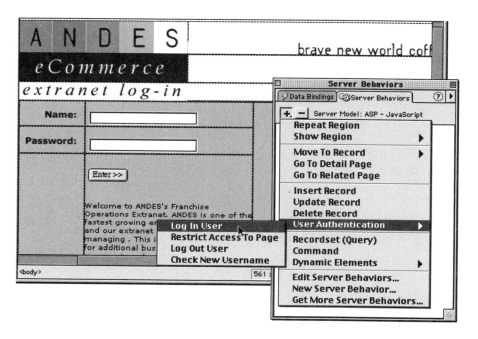

The Log In User dialog box will appear. You will need to make changes in three of the dialog box's four sections. The first section asks where to find user-supplied information. The second section asks where to find the data fields that match the first section's information. The third section asks where to send users who log in correctly or those who cannot log in; and the fourth section asks where the access level information is stored.

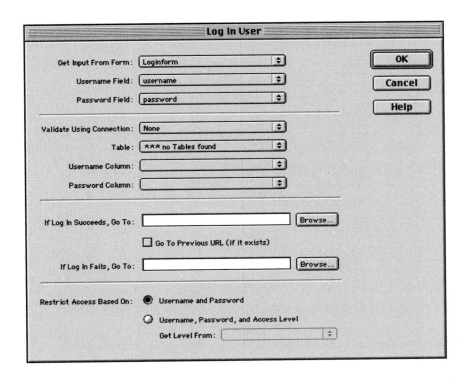

5) Leave the first section's settings as they are. In the second section, use the drop-down menus to set *Validate Using Connection* to *connAndes*, *Table* to *Customers*, *Username Column* to *Username*, and *Password Column* to *Password*.

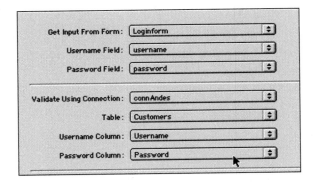

213

6) In the dialog box's third section, use the *Browse* buttons to set *If Log In Succeeds, Go To* to *product_search* and *If Log In Fails, Go To* to *andes_login_fail.html*.

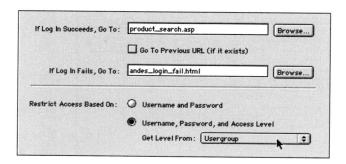

With these settings, users who successfully log in are sent to the site's home page, which is the product_search page. Users who cannot log in will see a simple HTML page explaining why they could not log in.

7) In the fourth section, choose the radio button for *Username, Password, and Access Level* and set the *Get Level From* drop-down menu to *Usergroup*.

The choices in this section set which items control the users' access. For example, you could require a password to log into the site but not apply page-level access restrictions.

8) Click *OK* to close the dialog box. Save the andes_login page, then move it—as well as the andes_login_fail.html page—to the remote server.

Click *Yes* when asked if you want to include dependent files, then close both pages.

9) Open the andes_login page in your Web browser, enter the name and password you noted in step 3, and click the *Enter* button.

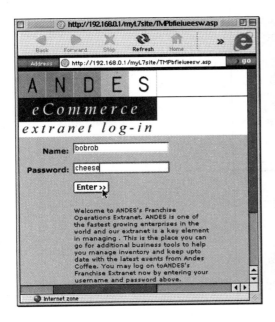

Your browser sends you to the product_search page, where you can begin searching for Andes products. In a successful login, two session variables are created: MM_Username, which holds the unique user name, and MM_UserAuthorization, which holds the user's access level. These two session variables allow the user to move to any other page on the site.

If you enter a name and password that are not in the database, you are sent to the andes_login_fail.html page. Clicking the *try again* link on that page sends you back to the login page, where you can enter an acceptable name-password pair.

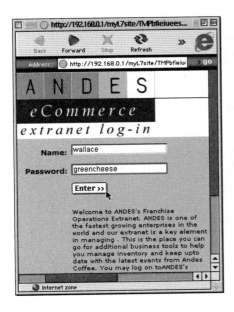

215

RESTRICTING LOGINS BY ACCESS LEVEL

In this task, you'll restrict which users can reach certain pages based on the user group to which they belong. The product_update page, which lets users change any product detail, is a good example of a page that you wouldn't necessarily let all users access.

1) Open the product_update page, click the + button in the Server Behaviors panel, and choose *User Authentication > Restrict Access To Page*.

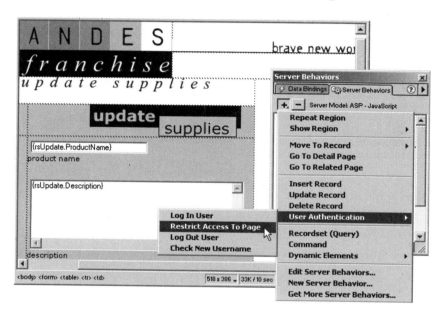

The Restrict Access To Page dialog box opens.

2) Select the *Username, Password, and Access Level* radio button and click the *Define* button.

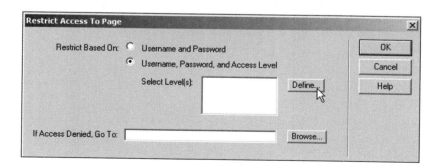

The Define Access Levels dialog box opens.

3) Type admin **as the *Name*, then click the** + **button to add it to the middle list window. Repeat these steps to add** user **and** foreign **to the list. Click** *OK* **to close the dialog box.**

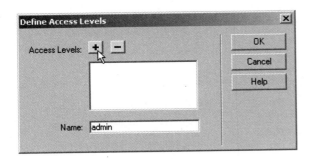

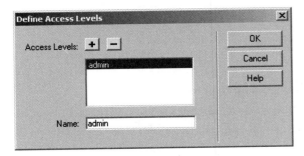

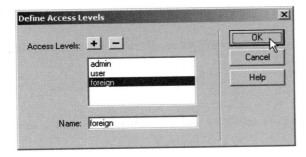

The Restrict Access To Page dialog box will reappear.

4) Click the *Browse* button, navigate to the *andes_admin_only.html* page, and select it.

When the Restrict Access To Page dialog box reappears, click *OK* to close it. By selecting the andes_admin_only.html page, unauthorized users will see an explanation on why they were blocked and sent to the product_detail page, which is open to all users.

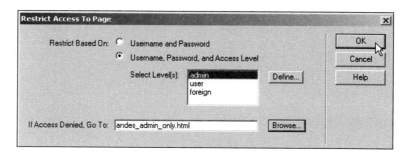

5) Save the page and repeat steps 1-4 for the product_add page.

Like the product_update page, the product_add page is not one that you want just any user to be able to access. When you open the page's Define Access Levels dialog box, you'll find that the three user values (*admin*, *user*, and *foreign*) have already been added for you.

6) Save the product_add page, then move it—as well as the product_update page—to the remote server.

Click *Yes* when asked if you want to include dependent files, then close both pages.

7) Open the andes_login page in your Web browser, enter jbates **as the *Name* and** pumpkin **as the *Password*, and click the *Enter* button.**

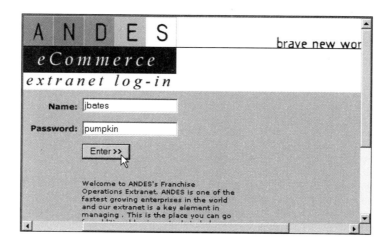

218

This name-password pair, which you noted in the previous task, has only a "user" access level.

8) Use your Web browser to go to a product page and click the *Update* button at the bottom.

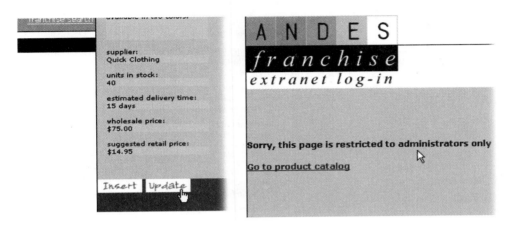

Because you have only a user access level, the browser sends you to the andes_admin_only.html page, which displays a message about why your access was blocked. Clicking a product page's *Insert* button, which links to the product_add page, will yield the same result.

RESTRICTING LOGINS BY PASSWORDS

Creating usergroup-based restrictions, as you did in the previous task, enables you to quickly define rights and permissions for many people at once. In this task, you'll restrict access based on individual logins, which enables you to fine-tune the rights and permissions for your site.

219

1) Open the product_detail page, click the + button in the **Server Behaviors** panel, and choose *User Authentication > Restrict Access To Page.*

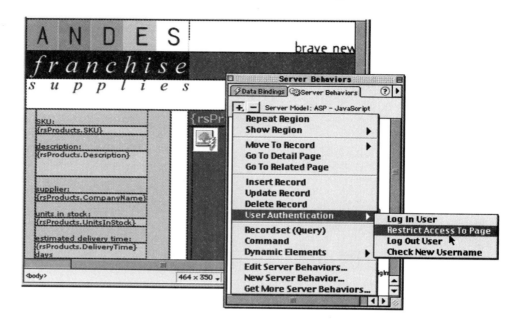

The Restrict Access To Page dialog box opens. Since the product_detail page simply displays product information, access to it need not be quite as restricted as the product_update and product_add pages.

TIP *The Username and Password radio button is selected by default. For this exercise, leave it selected.).*

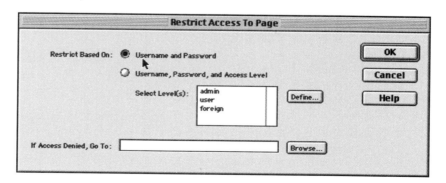

2) Click the *Browse* button, navigate to the *andes_access_denied.html* page, and select it. Save the page and move it to the remote server.

When the Restrict Access To Page dialog box reappears, click *OK* to close it. By selecting the andes_admin_only.html page, unauthorized users will see an explanation about why they were denied access.

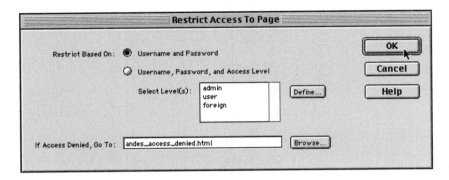

3) Repeat steps 1-2 for the product_search and product_resultlist pages.

You have now applied password-level restrictions to all three pages. In the next task, you'll get to use passwords to personalize the pages that users visit.

TIP *To reach these now-restricted pages with your Web browser, you'll need to start at the andes_login page and enter a name-password pair. Once you've logged in via your browser, you'll be able to move around the site as before. But if you quit your browser, flushing the temporarily cached site pages, you'll need to log in again at the andes_login page.*

PERSONALIZING PAGES FOR USERS

Once a user logs into the site, you can use the MM_Username session variable to personalize any page visited by that user. For example, you can modify the product_resultlist page to display something such as "Result of search for Coffee from any supplier on behalf of Bob." The procedure is remarkably easy.

1) Open the andes_login page, copy the *rsCustomers* recordset, then open the product_resultlist page and paste in the recordset.

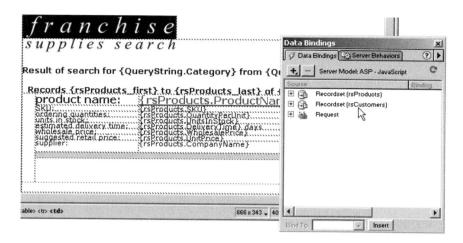

Use the right-click (Windows) or Control+click (Macintosh) trick to copy the recordset from the Data Bindings panel of one page to the other.

2) Double-click *Recordset(rsCustomers)* in the Data Bindings panel to reach the Recordset dialog box.

If the dialog box opens with the advanced form displayed, switch to the simple form by clicking the *Simple* button. (If the *Advanced* button is visible, you're already in the simple form.)

3) In the lower portion of the dialog box, set the *Filter* drop-down menu to *Username*, the upper-right drop-down menu to =, the lower-left drop-down menu to *Session Variable*, and type `MM_Username` **in the lower-right text field.**

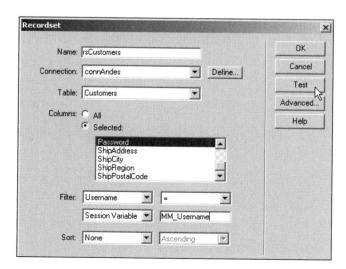

As you recall from earlier in this lesson, when a user logs in, a MM_Username session variable is created. That variable holds a unique user name. These settings filter the recordset based on that particular user name and, so, personalize pages.

4) Click the *Test* button, type into the *Test Value* text field one of the user names you noted earlier, and click *OK*.

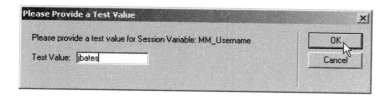

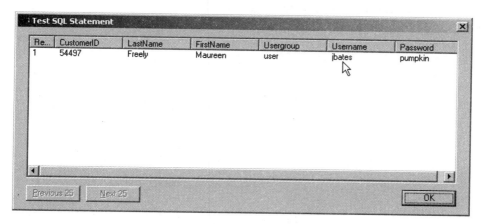

If you've set everything properly, the Test SQL Statement dialog box appears and displays the customer record for that particular user name.

5) Click *OK* to close the dialog box, click *OK* again to close the recordset dialog box. Type `on behalf of` **within the product_resultlist page, expand *Recordset(rsCustomers)* in the Data Bindings panel, and drag the *FirstName* field into place at the end of the phrase.**

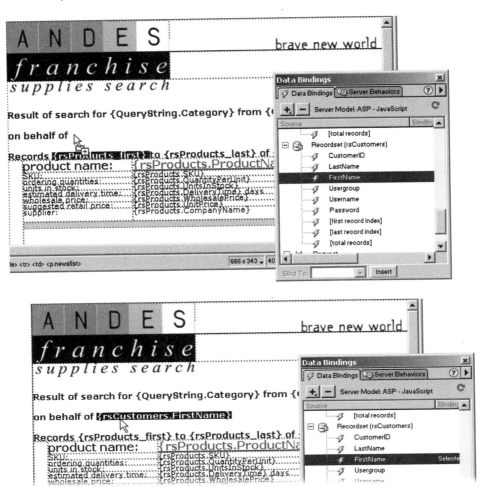

A placeholder for the *FirstName* data will be inserted on the page. Save the product_resultlist page and click the page's File Management button, and choose Put (Ctrl+Shift+U Windows, Command+Shift+U Macintosh) to move the file to the remote server. Click *Yes* when asked if you want to include dependent files.

6) Click the Preview in Browser button (F12).

When the page appears in your Web browser, the *on behalf of* phrase will include the user name you supplied when logging into the site. Obviously you don't need to construct this exact phrase and can instead use any of the rsCustomer data fields to personalize this or any other page for the user.

CHECKING NEW USER NAMES AGAINST EXISTING NAMES

When a new user logs into the site, the Check New Username server behavior in UltraDev's User Authentication group checks it against the Users data table and blocks the login if the name has already been taken by another user.

Rather than simply block such logins and leave users in the dark about what's happened, your site's Local Folder contains two predesigned pages to help them out : username_exists and andes_newuser. The first page, which will be displayed automatically whenever a login is blocked, explains that the user has chosen a name already being used and includes a link back to the login form so the user can enter another username. The second page offers the user the option of registering a new name by including a simplified registration form, the rsCustomers recordset, and the server behaviors needed to assign a user ID and insert that new record into the data table. In this task, you will add server behaviors to activate both the username_exists page and the andes_newuser page.

1) Open the andes_newuser page, click the + button in the Server Behaviors panel, and choose *User Authentication* > *Check New Username*.

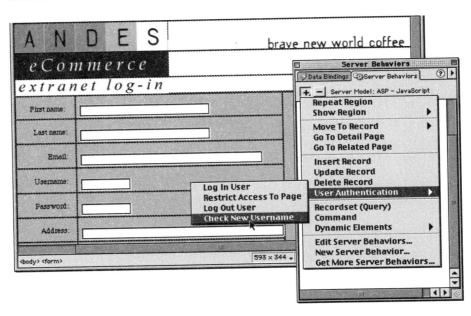

The Check New User dialog box opens.

2) Set the *Username Field* to *Username*, click the *Browse* button and navigate to your site's username_exists page. When the dialog box reappears, click *OK* to close it.

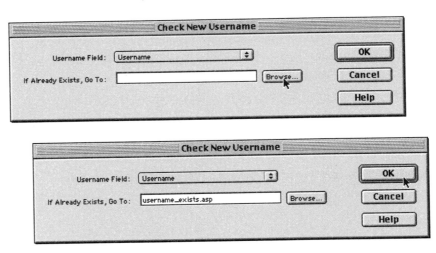

3) Close the username_exists page and save it.

4) Open the username_exists page, click the + button in the Data Bindings panel, and choose *Request Variable*.

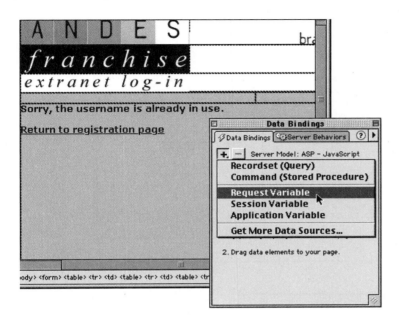

The Request Variable dialog box opens.

5) Type requsername **into the *Name* field and click *OK* to close the dialog box.**

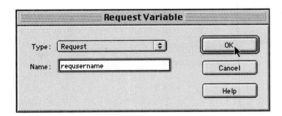

The dialog box's *Type* will already be set to *Request*.

6) Select *requsername* in the Data Bindings panel and drag it into the page between the words *username* and *is*.

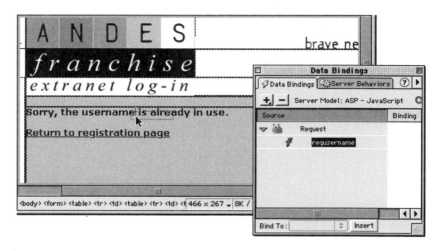

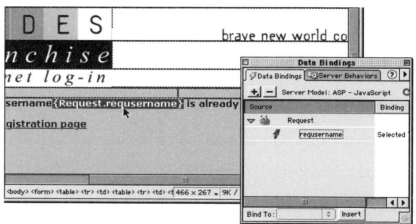

A placeholder for the requsername is inserted into the page.

7) Save the username_exists page, then move it—as well as the andes_newuser page—to the remote server. Click *Yes* when asked if you want to include dependent files, then close both pages.

You can test the pages by logging into the site with one browser, then attempting to log on from another computer using the same name-password pair. The username_exists page will be displayed in the second browser with a link back to the login page.

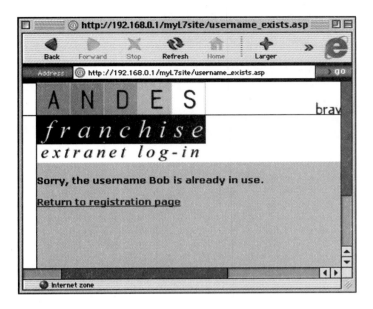

Inside the browser window:

@ http://192.168.0.1/myL7site/username_exists.asp

Back Forward Stop Refresh Home Larger »

Address @ http://192.168.0.1/myL7site/username_exists.asp › go

A N D E S

brav

franchise
extranet log-in

Sorry, the username Bob is already in use.

Return to registration page

Internet zone

WHAT YOU HAVE LEARNED

In this lesson, you have:

- Used a server behavior that authenticates users by checking their login name-password against data stored in an existing customers recordset (pages 210–215)

- Restricted access to certain pages based on users' access levels (as defined by the usergroup field in the customer recordset) and redirected unqualified users to a page explaining why their entry was blocked (pages 216–219)

- Blocked access to some site pages based on users' passwords (as defined by the username and password fields in the customer recordset) and redirected unqualified users to an explanatory page (pages 219–221)

- Checked a customer's username against the customer recordset and then displayed personalized pages based on that information (pages 221–225)

- Compared a user's name-password login against those already in use to prevent duplicate logins (pages 225–229)

building server behaviors

UltraDev ships with about two dozen built-in server behaviors. You've already used most of them in this book. Over 300 server behavior extensions—new server behaviors written by UltraDev enthusiasts within Macromedia and also out of house—are available for free download at the Macromedia Exchange Web site: www.macromedia.com/exchange/ultradev/. The most convenient way to get there is to connect to the Internet, click the + button in the Server Behaviors panel, and choose *Get More Server Behaviors* from the drop-down menu.

To get comfortable with UltraDev's Server Behavior Builder, you will learn how to add a date and timestamp to any page.

In this lesson, you also will build several simple server behaviors yourself, using UltraDev's built-in server behavior builder and editor. The code you need can be found within the file *sbcodes.html*.

WHAT YOU WILL LEARN

In this lesson, you will:

- Place session variables in the Data Bindings panel

- Build a simple server behavior based on those variables

- Build a more complex server behavior to write cookies to the user's browser

- Use the WriteCookies behavior to store a username and password

- Download a server behavior extension from the Macromedia Exchange

- Install the server behavior extension that you download

APPROXIMATE TIME

It usually takes about 90 minutes to complete this lesson.

LESSON FILES

Media Files:

none

Starting Files:

UltraDev 4 Lessons\...\Current files\sbcodes.html

UltraDev 4 Lessons\...\Current files\andes_login

UltraDev 4 Lessons\...\Current files\product_search

Completed Project:

Same as Starting Files

DISPLAYING SESSION VARIABLES

Before you can build a simple date/time server behavior, you first need to place both variable names in the Data Bindings panel so they can be displayed on your pages and in your data management operations. The first variable, today, will display a readable date in the format MM/DD/YY. The second variable, ts, will display a data timestamp representing elapsed milliseconds since 1/1/80. By the way, once a session variable is displayed in the Data Bindings panel on any page, it's available for building on every page of your site.

1) Open any page in your site, click the + button in the Data Bindings panel, and choose *Session Variable* from the drop-down menu.

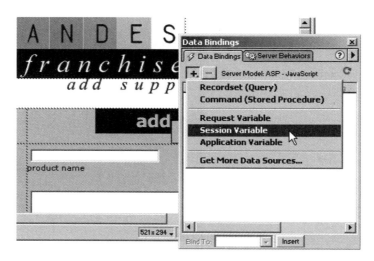

The Session Variable dialog box opens.

2) Type today **in the *Name* window and click *OK*.**

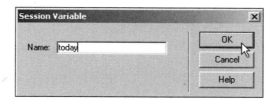

The Session Variable dialog box closes and the *today* variable is added to the Data Bindings panel.

3) Repeat step 1 and type ts **in the Session Variable dialog box's** *Name* **window and click** *OK.*

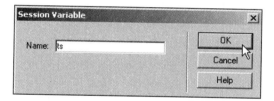

The *ts* variable is added to the Data Bindings panel, which you can see by clicking the + next to *Session.*

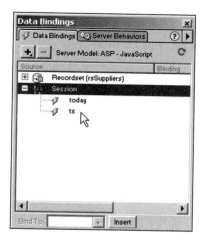

Neither variable has a defined value. That comes in the next task.

BUILDING A SIMPLE DATE/TIME SERVER BEHAVIOR

In building a Web site, you often need to display the current date or time on a page. No matter which server technology you are using, fairly simple source code is available to create date and time values—it's just a matter of formatting the values and making them available for use. In the previous task, you added the date and time variables to the Data Bindings panel so that they could be displayed on any page. Now you're going to build the date/time server behaviors and define their session variables for the andes_login page.

1) Open the sbcodes.html file in your site's *Local Folder*. Click the Code View button to see the file's code.

You need to select and copy the code for the *TodayTs* server behavior. Which code block you select depends on which server technology you're using.

If you're using ASP with JavaScript, the block begins with <% and ends with %> and appears just below <p class="articletext">ASP/JavaScript:</p>:

If you're using ASP with VBScript, the block begins with <% and ends with %> and appears just below <p class="articletext">ASP/VBScript:</p>:

If you're using ColdFusion, the block begins with <cfset Macromedia = and appears just below <p class="articletext">ColdFusion:</p>:

If you're using ASP with JSP, the block begins with <% and ends with %> and appears just below <p class="articletext">JSP:</p>:

TIP *While you can hunt down the necessary code in Code View and select it by hand, there's a much quicker—and more accurate—way. With the sbcodes.html file open, choose View > Visual Aids > Invisible Elements, then click the Code and Design View button.*

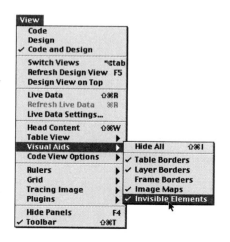
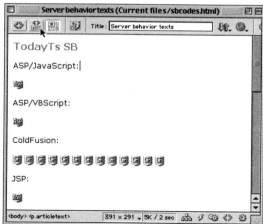

With the Server Behavior icons now visible, click the appropriate icon in the Design View, then copy it from the Code View window (Ctrl+C Windows, Command+C Mac).

The split Code and Design View lets you see exactly what code is selected whenever you click an icon. Once you've selected an icon in the lower Design View window, be sure to click in the upper Code View window before you copy. Otherwise, the code will not be copied. If you're using ColdFusion, be sure to select all nine element icons in the Design View window.

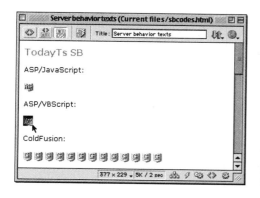
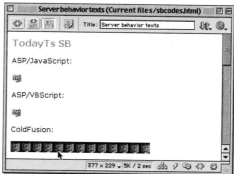

235

2) Once you find the code appropriate for your server technology, copy it to the clipboard (Ctrl+C Windows, Command+C Mac). Close the sbcodes.html file and open the andes_login page. Click the + button in the Server Behaviors panel and choose *New Server Behavior* from the drop-down menu.

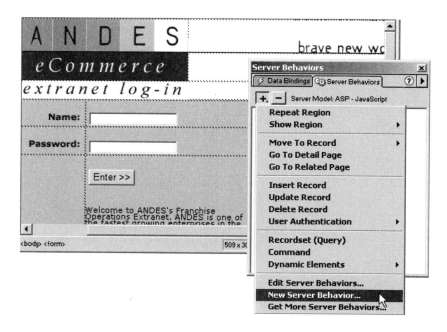

The New Server Behavior dialog box opens.

3) Set the *Server Model* drop-down menu to the server technology you are using, type TodayTs in the *Name* window, and click *OK* to close the dialog box.

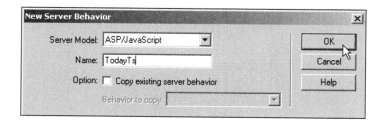

The Server Behavior Builder dialog box for the new TodayTs behavior will open.

4) Click the + button in the Server Behavior Builder dialog box.

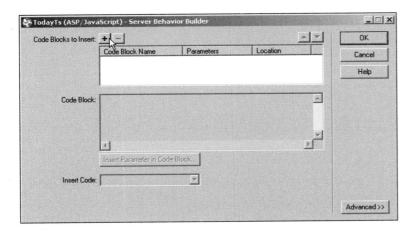

When the Create a New Code Block dialog box opens, *TodayTs_block1* automatically appears in the *Name* window.

5) Click *OK* to close the dialog box.

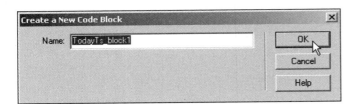

When the Server Behavior Builder dialog box reappears, *TodayTs_block1* will have been added to the *Code Blocks to Insert* list and a placeholder code block is highlighted in the *Code Block* window.

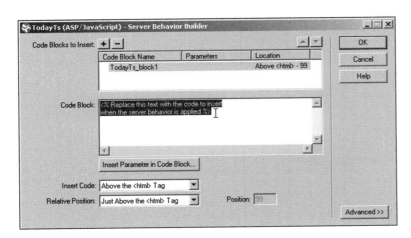

6) Replace the highlighted code by pasting in the code you copied in step 2 (Ctrl+V Windows, Command+V Mac).

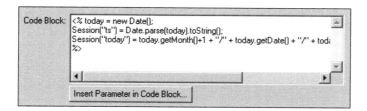

Now you need to decide where the server behavior builder will insert the code block. The dialog box offers several options for positioning the code block. The *Insert Code* drop-down menu controls whether the block is placed at the top or bottom of the document (*Above the <html> Tag* or *Below the </html> Tag*), relative to a specific tag, or relative to whatever element is selected on the page. The *Relative Position* drop-down menu lets you fine-tune the position based on your *Insert Code* menu choice.

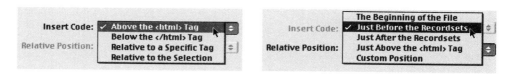

7) Set the *Insert Code* drop-down menu to *Above the <html> Tag* and the *Relative Position* menu to *Just Before the Recordsets*. Click *OK* to close the dialog box.

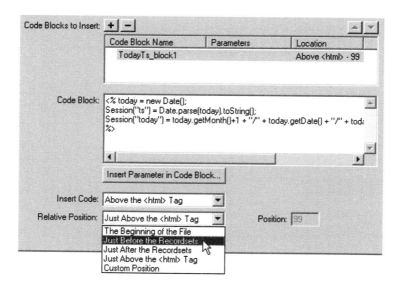

Code blocks that simply define the value of session variables should always be placed above the <html> tag. Placing this code block before the recordsets keeps things simple since then the code doesn't depend on the existence of an actual recordset.

8) Click the + button in the Server Behaviors panel and choose *TodayTs* from the drop-down menu.

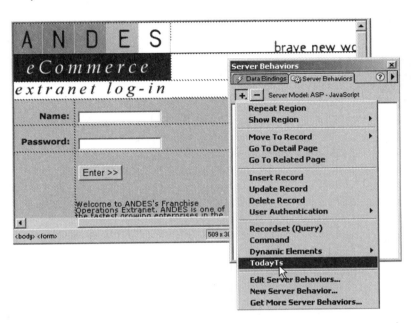

The new behavior is applied to the andes_login page. If you like, you can click the Code View button and see that the code has been inserted just above the source code for the *rsCustomers* recordset.

9) Save the andes_login page and transfer it to the server.

Click *Yes* when asked if you want to include dependent files.

10) Open the product_search page and using the *normaltextunleaded* CSS style, type Date: **and** Timestamp: **on separate lines just above the *category* menu.**

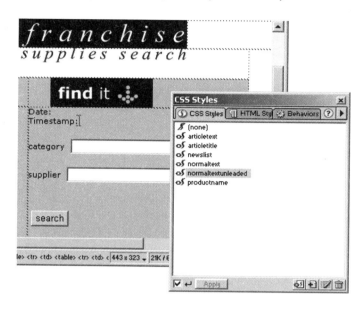

Insert a line break between *Date:* and *Timestamp:* (Shift+Enter Windows, Command+ Return Mac).

11) Expand the Session list in the Data Bindings panel and drag *today* to a spot right after *Date:* and *ts* right after *Timestamp:*.

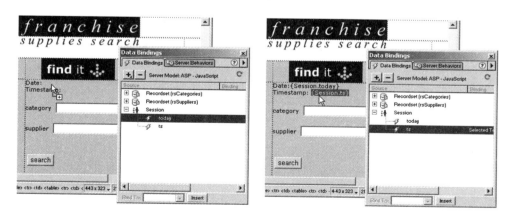

240

12) Save the product_search page and transfer it to the server.

Click *Yes* when asked if you want to include dependent files. When you log into the site with your Web browser and open the product_search page, the date and time will appear.

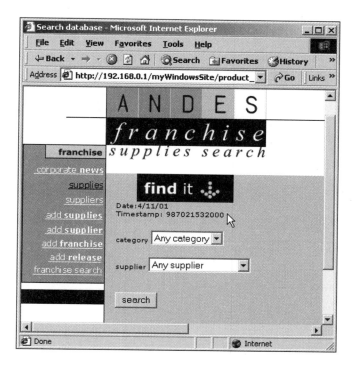

This server behavior was relatively simple to create because it didn't need any values from the user. The next task, which uses a cookie, shows you how to gather parameters from the user for more elaborate behaviors.

BUILDING A SERVER BEHAVIOR TO WRITE COOKIES

Practically all of the built-in server behaviors in UltraDev launch some sort of dialog box when you select them. The information you type (or select) in the dialog box constitutes the behavior's parameters. Parameters usually have different values every time a behavior is applied, as opposed to the fixed code blocks used in the previous task, which do not change.

You are going to build a server behavior to write a cookie, which will need three parameters: the name of the cookie (called the Cookiename), the value of the cookie (Cookievalue), and the cookie's expiration time in days (Cookieexpire).

These three parameter names can be found in the source code of the sbcodes.html file. Once again, which bit of code you select depends on your server model.

1) Open the sbcodes.html file and click the Code and View button.

If the Server Behavior icons are not visible on the page, choose View > Visual Aids > Invisible Elements.

2) Select the *WriteCookie SB* icon that matches your server model in the View window and then copy it from the Code window (Ctrl+C Windows, Command+C Mac).

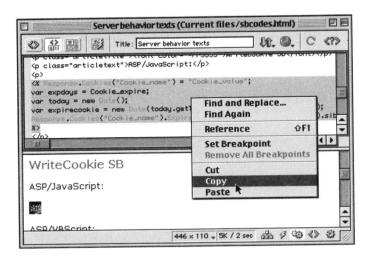

As in the previous task, you can click the Code and Design View button if you want to see the actual code as you select it.

3) Close the sbcodes.html file and reopen the product_search page. Click the + button in the Server Behaviors panel and choose *New Server Behavior* from the drop-down menu.

The New Server Behavior dialog box will open.

4) Set the *Server Model* drop-down menu to the server technology you are using, type `WriteCookies` in the *Name* field, and click *OK* to close the dialog box.

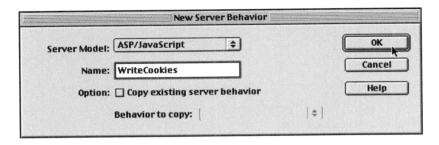

The Server Behavior Builder dialog box will open.

5) Click the + button in the Server Behavior Builder dialog box.

WriteCookies_block1 automatically appears in the *Name* field of the Create a New Code Block dialog box.

6) Click *OK* to close the dialog box. Replace the code in the *Code Block* field with the code you copied in step 2.

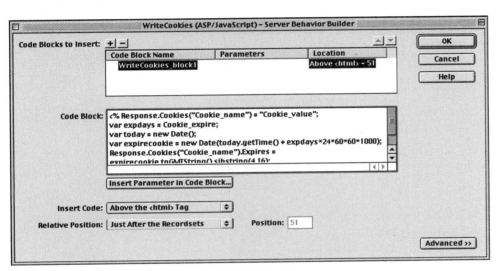

You're now ready to supply the three parameters needed for the WriteCookie behavior to work. Look in the *Code Block* field and you'll see the three parameter placeholders you'll be replacing: *Cookie_name*, *Cookie_value*, and *Cookie_expire*. UltraDev won't let you replace them with identically named parameters, so you'll be using slightly different names: Cookiename, Cookievalue, and Cookieexpire.

7) Use your cursor to select the first occurrence of *Cookie_name* (don't select the surrounding " ") in the *Code Block* field and click the *Insert Parameter in Code Block* button.

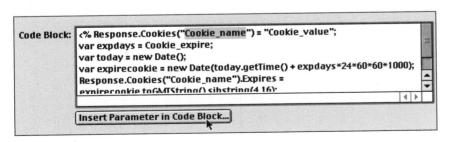

8) Type Cookiename **in the** *Parameter Name* **field of the dialog box and click** *OK*.

Insert Parameter In Code Block

A parameter is a placeholder in the code block for
information that will be specified when the behavior is
applied.

Parameter Name: Param1

[OK]
[Cancel]
[Help]

Insert Parameter In Code Block

A parameter is a placeholder in the code block for
information that will be specified when the behavior is
applied.

Parameter Name: Cookiename

[OK]
[Cancel]
[Help]

When the Server Behavior Builder dialog box reappears, *@@Cookiename@@* should
have replaced the Cookie_name placeholder in both places where it previously
appeared. If it does not replace the second placeholder (the Windows and Mac
versions of UltraDev behave differently on this), select it by hand and repeat steps 7
and 8. UltraDev uses double @ marks to mark parameters—making them easy to
spot in raw code.

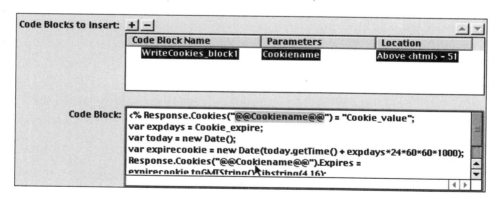

Code Blocks to Insert: [+] [–]

Code Block Name	Parameters	Location
WriteCookies_block1	Cookiename	Above <html> - 51

Code Block:
```
<% Response.Cookies("@@Cookiename@@") = "Cookie_value";
var expdays = Cookie_expire;
var today = new Date();
var expirecookie = new Date(today.getTime() + expdays*24*60*60*1000);
Response.Cookies("@@Cookiename@@").Expires =
expirecookie.toGMTString().substring(4,16);
```

9) Repeat steps 7 and 8, except this time select *Cookie_value* and replace it with *Cookievalue*.

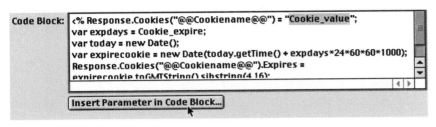

Code Block:
```
<% Response.Cookies("@@Cookiename@@") = "Cookie_value";
var expdays = Cookie_expire;
var today = new Date();
var expirecookie = new Date(today.getTime() + expdays*24*60*60*1000);
Response.Cookies("@@Cookiename@@").Expires =
expirecookie toGMTString() sihstring(4 16).
```

[Insert Parameter in Code Block...]

Insert Parameter In Code Block

A parameter is a placeholder in the code block for information that will be specified when the behavior is applied.

Parameter Name: `Cookievalue`

[OK] [Cancel] [Help]

Code Block Name	Parameters	Location
WriteCookies_block1	Cookiename, Cookievalue	Above <html> – 51

Code Block:
```
<% Response.Cookies("@@Cookiename@@") = "@@Cookievalue@@";
var expdays = Cookie_expire;
var today = new Date();
var expirecookie = new Date(today.getTime() + expdays*24*60*60*1000);
Response.Cookies("@@Cookiename@@").Expires =
expirecookie toGMTString() sihstring(4 16).
```

This supplies the second of the three parameters you need. Notice that both parameters now appear in the *Parameters* column of the Server Behavior Builder dialog box's top field.

10) Repeat steps 7 and 8, selecting *Cookie_expire* and replacing it with *Cookieexpire*.

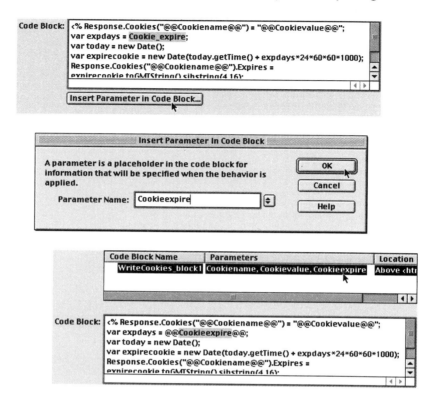

All three parameters now are listed in the dialog box's *Parameters* column.

11) Make sure the *Insert Code* drop-down menu is set to *Above the ‹html› Tab* and that the *Relative Position* menu is set to *Just After the Recordsets*, then click *Next*.

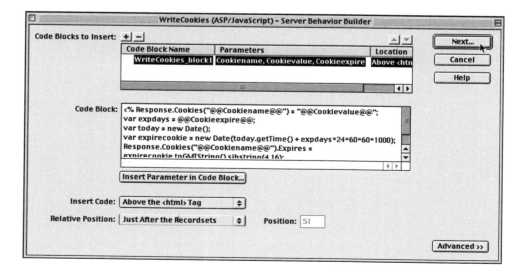

246

The Generate Behavior dialog box appears, listing each parameter. Use the arrow icons to rearrange the parameters to correspond to their order in the code: *Cookiename* first, *Cookievalue* second, and *Cookieexpire* last. Click *OK* to close the dialog box.

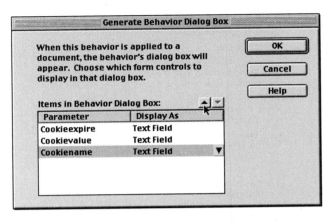

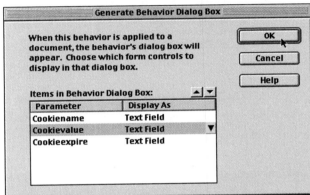

While you've generated the Writecookies behavior, you still have one remaining task: to set the behavior so that it stores the user's name and password

USING THE WRITECOOKIES BEHAVIOR
TO STORE A NAME AND PASSWORD

A common use of a cookie is to store a username–password combination. If the username and password are contained in a cookie—and the user doesn't delete the cookie—the user never again needs to remember which name and password to use for the site.

While this task creates username and password cookies for a specific user, in real-world practice the cookie values would be pulled from request variables supplied by the user during login. The point here is to give you a hands-on sense of how to use and modify the WriteCookies behavior for your own needs.

1) Open the product_search page, click the + button in the Server Behaviors panel and choose *WriteCookies*, the new behavior you created in the previous task.

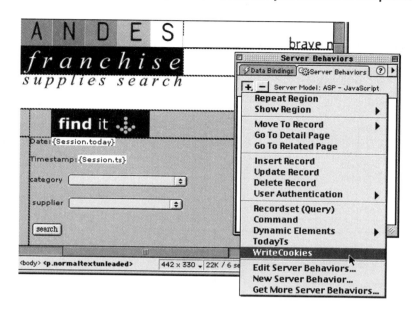

The WriteCookies dialog box opens. This is where you need to specify the cookie's name, value, and when it expires. Once you're done, these specifications will work with the three parameters you created in the previous task.

2) Type username **into the *Cookiename* text field,** bobrob **in the *Cookievalue* text field, and however many days you want the cookie to last into the *Cookieexpire* text field. Click *OK* to close the dialog box.**

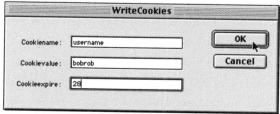

248

For consistency, the same username–password pair used Lesson 10, *bobrob* and *cheese*, is used in this task. It doesn't matter which pair you use—just as long as it exists in the rsCustomer recordset. The Cookieexpire value is set at *28* since a month is a fairly standard time to leave a cookie active.

3) Repeat step 1 and create a second cookie to handle a password by typing password **in the *Cookiename* text field,** cheese **in the *Cookievalue* text field and** 28 **in *Cookieexpire* text field. Click *OK* to close the dialog box.**

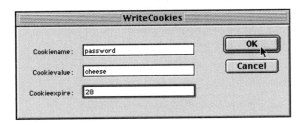

After filling out and closing both WriteCookies dialog boxes, both behavior variables appear in the Server Behavior panel. The next step is to bind each variable to its respective form field on the login page.

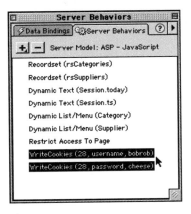

4) Save and close the product_search page, open the andes_login page, click the **+** button in the Data Bindings panel, and choose *Request Variable*.

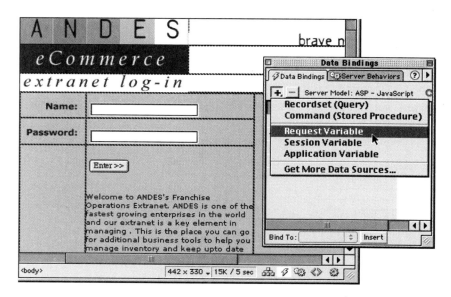

The Request Variable dialog box opens.

5) Set the *Type* drop-down menu to *Request.Cookie*, type username into the *Name* field, and click *OK* to close the dialog box.

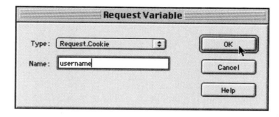

6) Select the *Name* text field on the andes_login page and the *Cookies.username* variable in the Data Bindings panel, then click the *Bind* button.

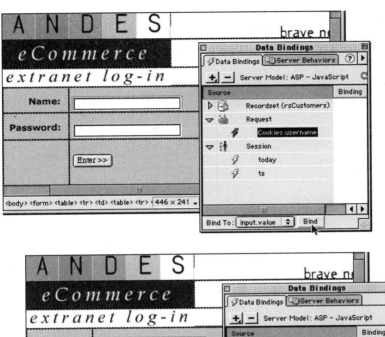

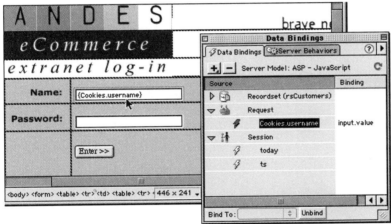

A *Cookies.username* placeholder appears in the *Name* field, indicating that the request variable has been bound to the form's text field.

7) Repeat steps 4-6, except type `password` **into the Request Variable *Name* field, and bind the *Cookies.password* value to the *Password* form field on the andes_login page.**

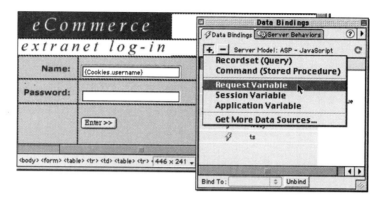

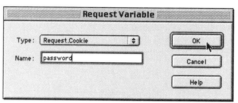

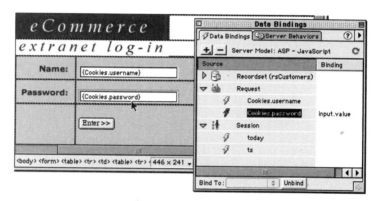

8) Save the andes_login page, then move it—as well as the product_search page to the remote server. Click *Yes* when asked if you want to include dependent files, then close both pages.

9) Log in to the site with your Web browser, view the product_search page, and quit your browser.

Whenever you next open the login page with your browser, the page's username and password information will be preset by the cookies previously written to your browser's cache.

DOWNLOADING EXTENSIONS

As you discovered in the previous tasks, extensions make UltraDev even more powerful. The Macromedia Exchange contains hundreds of free extensions and UltraDev's built-in Extension Manager makes it easy to download those you find of interest.

1) Connect to the Web, open any page on your site, and choose Commands > Manage Extensions.

The Macromedia Extension Manager will open.

2) Choose File > Go To Macromedia Exchange.

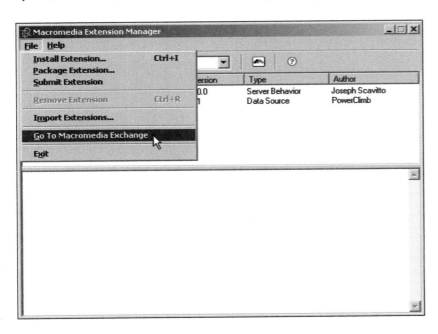

The Extension Manager will launch your Web browser and connect to the Exchange home page.

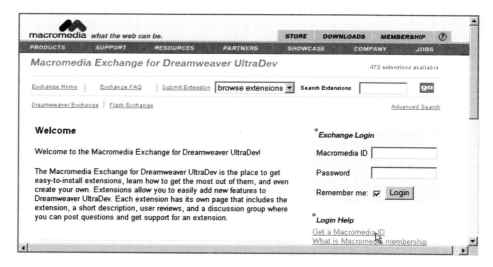

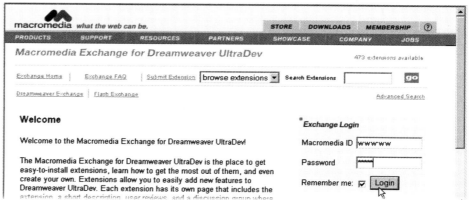

If it's your first visit to any of Macromedia's support forums, click the *Get a Macromedia ID* link and register. An ID and password will be emailed to you. Once you receive it, you can log into the Exchange. If you've previously logged in and checked the *Remember me* box, your browser will log you in automatically.

3) After logging in, use the *browse extensions* drop-down menu or the *Search Extensions* text field to look for extensions that interest you.

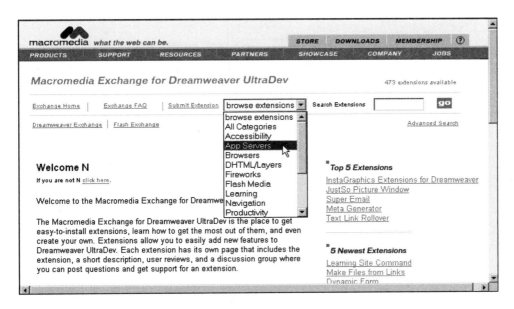

Extensions are grouped by function to make it easier to find what you need among the hundreds of available.

4) Once you find an extension, click its icon to download it.

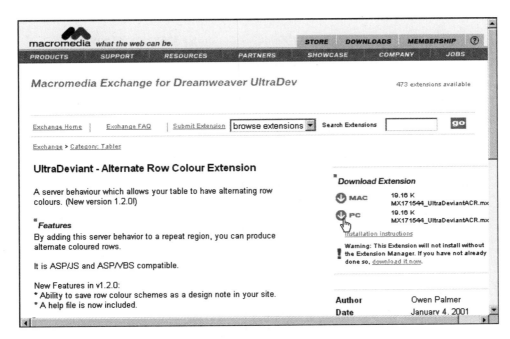

5) Navigate the series of dialog boxes that appear to save the extension to .../UltraDev 4 Lessons/DW-UDextensions/. Click *Save*.

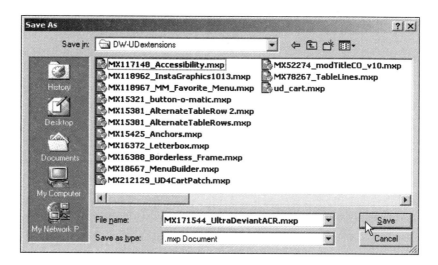

Once the extension downloads, log off the Web. In the next step, you'll learn how to install your new extension so that UltraDev can use it.

INSTALLING AN EXTENSION

As you'll see, installing an extension is easy. With new extensions being posted to the Macromedia Exchange constantly, you'll want to check the Macromedia Exchange regularly for other extensions you may find useful.

1) Open any page on your site and choose Commands > Manage Extensions.
The Macromedia Extension Manager will open.

2) Choose File > Install Extensions or (in the Windows version only) click the manager's Install button.

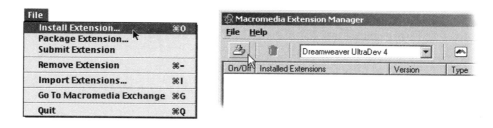

The Select Extension to Install (Windows) or Install Extension (Mac) dialog box will open.

3) Navigate to .../UltraDev 4 Lessons/DW-UDextensions, open the folder, select *ud_cart.mxp*, and click the *Install* button (*Open* on the Macintosh).

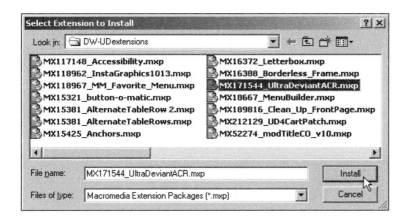

A disclaimer dialog box will appear, explaining that you are about to install a third-party extension. Read the fine print if you like, then click *Accept* and the extension will be installed.

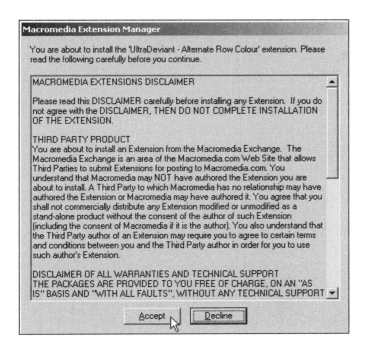

4) Once the installation is finished, another dialog box will appear telling you that you must quit UltraDev and restart it before the extension will be available. Click *OK*.

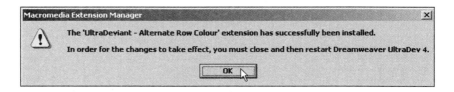

The new extension will appear in the Extension Manager.

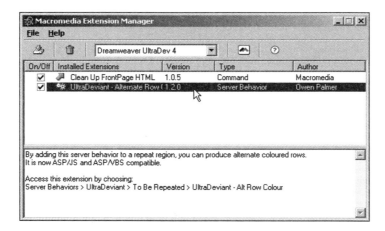

5) Quit the Extension Manager, then quit and relaunch UltraDev. Open any page once UltraDev restarts and click the + button in the Server Behaviors panel.

Your new server behavior will be available for use.

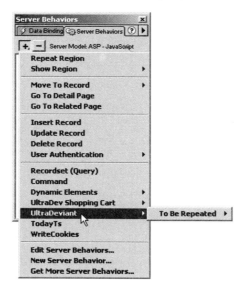

You can now begin using the extension to add new functions and behaviors to your UltraDev sites. By the way, when you install an extension that is not a server behavior, you use it by selecting it in the Commands menu.

WHAT YOU HAVE LEARNED

In this lesson, you have:

- Placed two session variables—one for date, one for elapsed time—in the Data Bindings panel so that they could be used in building the TodayTs server behavior (pages 232–233)

- Built a simple server behavior to display the date and time by copying pre-built code for a combined TodayTs server behavior (pages 233–241)

- Built a multiple-parameter server behavior to gather three values from users (pages 242–247)

- Used the multiple-parameter WriteCookies server behavior to write a username and password to the user's browser (pages 247–252)

- Logged onto the Macromedia Exchange, registered, and then downloaded a server behavior extension (pages 253–256)

- Installed and activated the server behavior extension you downloaded from the Macromedia Exchange (pages 256–259)

keyboard shortcuts

These keyboard-based commands are organized largely by function or topic. However, each table also lists the UltraDev menu where you'll find the shortcut so that you don't have to hunt it down yourself. Most of the commands apply equally to Dreamweaver or UltraDev. Commands found only in UltraDev are marked with an asterisk (*) with the most used UltraDev command categories listed first.

OPENING AND CLOSING PALETTES, PANELS, AND WINDOWS

Show/Hide	Windows	Macintosh	In Menu
All Panels	F4	F4	Window
Objects	Ctrl+F2	Command+F2	Window
Properties	Ctrl+F3	Command+F3	Window
Data Bindings*	Ctrl+F10	Command+F10	Window
Server Behaviors*	Ctrl+F9	Command+F9	Window
Site Files	F8	F8	Window
Site Map	Alt+F8	Option+F8	Window
Assets	F11	F11	Window
Behaviors	Shift+F3	Shift+F3	Window
Code inspector	F10	F10	Window
CSS Styles	Shift+F11	Shift+F11	Window
Frames	Shift+F2	Shift+F2	Window
History	Shift+F10	Shift+F10	Window
HTML Styles	Ctrl+F11	Command+F11	Window
Layers	F2	F2	Window
Reference	Ctrl+Shift+F1	Command+Shift+F1	Window
Timelines	Shift+F9	Shift+F9	Window
Minimize all windows	Shift+F4	n/a	Window
Restore all windows	Alt+Shift+F4	n/a	Window

SEEING PAGE VIEWS AND ELEMENTS

To Show/Hide	Windows	Macintosh	In Menu
Standard view	Ctrl+Shift+F6	Command+Shift+F6	View
Layout view	Ctrl+F6	Command+F6	View
Toolbar	Ctrl+Shift+T	Command+Shift+T	View
Design/Code views	Ctrl+Tab	Option+Tab	View
Refresh Design view*	F5	F5	View
Live Data view*	Ctrl+Shift+R	Command+Shift+R	View
Refresh Live Data view*	Ctrl+ R	Command+R	View
Visual Aids	Ctrl+Shift+I	Command+Shift+I	View
Rulers	Ctrl+Alt+R	Command+Option+R	View
Grid	Ctrl+Alt+G	Command+Option+G	View
Snap to Grid	Ctrl+Alt+Shift+G	Command+Option+Shift+G	View
Head content	Ctrl+Shift+W	Command+Shift+W	View
Page properties	Ctrl+J	Command+J	Modify
Selection properties	Ctrl+Shift+J	Command+Shift+J	Modify

MANAGING SITES AND FTP

Action	Windows	Macintosh	In Menu
Create new file	Ctrl+Shift+N	Command+Shift+N	File
Create new folder	Ctrl+Shift+Alt+N	Command+Shift+Option+N	File
Open selection	Ctrl+Shift+Alt+O	Command+Shift+Option+O	File
Get files/folders from FTP site	Ctrl+Shift+D	Command+Shift+D	Site
Put files/folders to FTP site	Ctrl+Shift+U	Command+Shift+U	Site
View site map	Alt+F8	Option+F8	Window & Site
View site files	F8	F8	Window & Site
Refresh remote site	Alt+F5	Option+F5	Site
Refresh Local Folder pane	Shift+F5	Shift+F5	Site
View as root	Ctrl+Shift+R	Command+Shift+R	Site
Link to existing file	Ctrl+Shift+K	Command+Shift+K	Site
Change link	Ctrl+L	Command+L	Modify
Remove link	Delete	Delete	Modify
Show/Hide links	Ctrl+Shift+Y	Command+Shift+Y	none
Show page titles	Ctrl+Shift+T	Command+Shift+T	none
Rename file	F2	n/a	none
Add items to library	Ctrl+Shift+B	Command+Shift+B	Modify
Zoom in site map	Ctrl+ + (plus)	Command+ + (plus)	none7
Zoom out site map	Ctrl+ − (hyphen)	Command+ − (hyphen)	none

262

MANAGING HYPERLINKS

Action	Windows	Macintosh	In Menu
Link selected text	Ctrl+L	Command+L	none
Remove hyperlink	Ctrl+Shift+L	Command+Shift+L	none
Open linked-to document	Ctrl-double-click link	Command-double-click link	none
Check links selected	Shift+F8	Shift+F8	File
Check all site links	Ctrl+F8	Command+F8	Site

PREVIEWING & DEBUGGING IN BROWSERS

Action	Windows	Macintosh	In Menu
Preview in primary browser	F12	F12	File
Preview in secondary browser	Ctrl+F12	Command+F12	File
Debug in primary browser	Alt+F12	Option+F12	File
Debug in secondary browser	Ctrl+Alt+F12	Command+Option+F12	File

MANAGING FILES AND ACTIONS

Action	Windows	Macintosh	In Menu
New document	Ctrl+N	Command+N	File
Open HTML file	Ctrl+O	Command+O	File
Open in frame	Ctrl+Shift+O	Command+Shift+O	File
Close	Ctrl+W	Command+W	File
Save	Ctrl+S	Command+S	File
Save as	Ctrl+Shift+S	Command+Shift+S	File
Check links	Shift+F8	Command+F8	File
Exit/Quit	Ctrl+Q	Command+Q	File
Undo	Ctrl+Z	Command+Z	Edit
Redo	Ctrl+Y or Ctrl+Shift+Z	Command+Y or Command+Shift+Z	Edit
Cut	Ctrl+X or Shift+Del	Command+X or Shift+Del	Edit
Copy	Ctrl+C or Ctrl+Insert	Command+C or Command+Insert	Edit
Copy HTML*	Shift+Ctrl+C	Shift+Command+C	Edit
Paste	Ctrl+V or Shift+Insert	Command+V or Shift+Insert	Edit
Paste HTML*	Shift+Ctrl+V	Shift+Command+V	Edit
Clear	Delete	Delete	Edit
Select All	Ctrl+A	Command+A	Edit
Select parent tag	Ctrl+Shift+‹	Command+Shift+‹	Edit
Select child tag	Ctrl+Shift+›	Command+Shift+›	Edit
Find and Replace	Ctrl+F	Command+F	Edit
Find next	F3	Command+G	Edit
Launch External Editor	Ctrl+E	Command+E	Edit
Preferences	Ctrl+U	Command+U	Edit

SELECTING & NAVIGATING

Select/Move To	Windows	Macintosh	In Menu
All	Ctrl+A	Command+A	Edit
Non-contiguous items	Ctrl+click	Command+click	none
Select line up	Shift+Up	Shift+Up	none
Select line down	Shift+Down	Shift+Down	none
Select character left	Shift+Left	Shift+Left	none
Select character right	Shift+Right	Shift+Right	none
Select to page up	Shift+Page Up	Shift+Page Up	none
Select to page down	Shift+Page Down	Shift+Page Down	none
Move to page up	Page Up	Page Up	none
Move to page down	Page Down	Page Down	none
Select a word	Double-click	Double-click	none
Select word left	Ctrl+Shift+Left	Command+Shift+Left	none
Select word right	Ctrl+Shift+Right	Command+Shift+Right	none
Select parent tag	Ctrl+Shift+‹	Command+Shift+‹	none
Move to start of line	Home	Home	none
Move to end of line	End	End	none
Select to top of code	Ctrl+Shift+Home	Command+Shift+Home	none
Select to end of code	Ctrl+Shift+End	Command+Shift+End	none
Move to top of code	Ctrl+Home	Command+Home	none
Move to end of code	Ctrl+End	Command+End	none
Select parent tag	Ctrl+Shift+‹	Command+Shift+‹	Edit
Select child tag	Ctrl+Shift+›	Command+Shift+›	Edit
Select table	Ctrl+A in table	Command+A in table	Modify
Move to next cell	Tab	Tab	none
Move to previous cell	Shift+Tab	Shift+Tab	none
Select layer	Ctrl+Shift-click	Command+Shift-click	none
Select frame	Alt-click frame	Shift+Option-click frame	none
Select next frame/frameset	Alt+Right Arrow	Command+Right Arrow	none
Select previous frame/frameset	Alt+Left Arrow	Command+Left Arrow	none
Select parent frameset	Alt+Up Arrow	Command+Up Arrow	none
Select first child frame/frameset	Alt+Down Arrow	Command+Down Arrow	none

264

EDITING CODE

Action	Windows	Macintosh	In Menu
Open Quick Tag Editor	Ctrl+T	Command+T	Modify
Select parent tag	Ctrl+Shift+<	Command+Shift+<	Edit
Indent Code	Ctrl+Shift+]	Command+Shift+]	Edit
Outdent Code	Ctrl+Shift+[	Ctrl+Shift+[	Edit
Balance Braces	Ctrl+'	Command+'	Edit
Toggle Breakpoint	Ctrl+Alt+B	Command+Option+B	Edit
Move to start of line	Home	Home	none
Move to end of line	End	End	none
Move to top of code	Ctrl+Home	Command+Home	none
Move to end of code	Ctrl+End	Command+End	none
Select to top of code	Ctrl+Shift+Home	Command+Shift+Home	none
Select to end of code	Ctrl+Shift+End	Command+Shift+End	none

EDITING & FORMATTING TEXT

Action	Windows	Macintosh	In Menu
Create a new paragraph	Enter	Return	none
Insert line break	Shift+Enter	Shift+Return	Modify
Insert nonbreaking space	Ctrl+Shift+Spacebar	Option+Spacebar	Modify
Select a word	Double-click	Double-click	none
Toggle design/code views	Ctrl+Tab	Option+Tab	View
Open/close Property inspector	Ctrl+F3	Command+F3	Window
Check spelling	Shift+F7	Shift+F7	Text
Indent	Ctrl+]	Command+]	Text
Outdent	Ctrl+[	Command+[	Text
Format > None	Ctrl+0 (zero)	Command+0 (zero)	Text
Paragraph Format	Ctrl+Shift+P	Command+Shift+P	Text
Apply Headings 1-6	Ctrl+1 through 6	Command+1 through 6	Text
Align to Left	Ctrl+Shift+Alt+L	Command+Shift+Option+L	Text
Align to Center	Ctrl+Shift+Alt+C	Command+Shift+Option+C	Text
Align to Right	Ctrl+Shift+Alt+R	Command+Shift+Option+R	Text
Bold selection	Ctrl+B	Command+B	Text
Italicize selection	Ctrl+I	Command+I	Text
Edit Style Sheet	Ctrl+Shift+E	Command+Shift+E	Text
Find Text	Ctrl+F	Command+F	Edit
Find Next/Find Again	F3	Command+G	Edit
Replace Text	Ctrl+H	Command+H	Edit

EDITING & FORMATTING TABLES

Action	Windows	Macintosh	In Menu
Select table	Ctrl+A	Command+A	Modify
Move to next cell	Tab	Tab	none
Move to previous cell	Shift+Tab	Shift+Tab	none
Insert row above selection	Ctrl+M	Command+M	Insert
Add row at end of table	Tab in last cell	Tab in last cell	Modify
Delete current row	Ctrl+Shift+M	Command+Shift+M	Modify
Insert column	Ctrl+Shift+A	Command+Shift+A	Modify
Delete column	Ctrl+Shift+ – (hyphen)	Command+Shift+ – (hyphen)	Modify
Merge selected cells	Ctrl+Alt+M	Command+Option+M	Modify
Split cells	Ctrl+Alt+S	Command+Option+S	Modify
Update table layout	Ctrl+Spacebar	Command+Spacebar	none

FORMATTING FRAMES

Action	Windows	Macintosh	In Menu
Select frame	Alt-click in frame	Shift+Option-click in frame	none
Select next frame/frameset	Alt+Right Arrow	Command+Right Arrow	none
Select previous frame/frameset	Alt+Left Arrow	Command+Left Arrow	none
Select parent frameset	Alt+Up Arrow	Command+Up Arrow	none
Select first child frame/frameset	Alt+Down Arrow	Command+Down Arrow	none
Add frame	Alt-drag frame border	Option-drag frame border	none
Add frame (push method)	Alt+Ctrl-drag frame border	Command+Option-drag frame border	none

WORKING WITH LAYERS

Action	Windows	Macintosh	In Menu
Select layer	Ctrl+Shift-click	Command+Shift-click	none
Select and move layer	Shift+Ctrl-drag	Command+Shift-drag	none
Add/Remove layer	Shift-click layer	Shift-click layer	none
Move layer by pixels	Arrow keys	Arrow keys	none
Move layer by snap increment	Shift+arrow keys	Shift+arrow keys	none
Resize selected layer by pixels	Ctrl+Arrow keys	Option+arrow keys	none
Resize layer by snap increment	Ctrl+Shift+arrow keys	Option+Shift+arrow keys	none
Align selected layers to Top/Bottom/Left/Right of last selected layer	Ctrl+Arrow keys	Command+Arrow keys	none
Make selected layers same width	Ctrl+Shift+[	Command+Shift+[	none
Make selected layers same height	Ctrl+Shift+]	Command+Shift+]	none
Toggle nesting preference on/off	Ctrl-drag	Command-drag	none
Show/Hide grid	Ctrl+Shift+Alt+G	Command+Shift+Option+G	none
Snap To grid	Ctrl+Alt+G	Command+Option+G	none

WORKING WITH IMAGES

Action	Windows	Macintosh	In Menu
Insert image	Ctrl+Alt+I	Command+Option+I	Insert
Change image attribute	Double-click image	Double-click image	none
Edit with external editor	Ctrl+double-click image	Command+double-click image	none

INSERTING OBJECTS

Action	Windows	Macintosh	In Menu
Image	Ctrl+Alt+I	Command+Option+I	Insert
Table	Ctrl+Alt+T	Command+Option+T	Insert
Flash movie	Ctrl+Alt+F	Command+Option+F	Insert
Shockwave Director movie	Ctrl+Alt+D	Command+Option+D	Insert
Named anchor	Ctrl+Alt+A	Command+Option+A	Insert

PLAYING PLUGINS

Action	Windows	Macintosh	In Menu
Play plugin	Ctrl+Alt+P	Command+Option+P	View
Stop plugin	Ctrl+Alt+X	Command+Option+X	View
Play all plugins	Ctrl+Shift+Alt+P	Command+Shift+Option+P	View
Stop all plugins	Ctrl+Shift+Alt+X	Command+Shift+Option+X	View

connecting macintoshes to a windows server

As noted in Lesson 2, if you're using UltraDev with a Macintosh client machine, you'll need to use either a Windows NT server or Windows 2000 Server running Internet Information Server (IIS). If IIS is not already installed on the server, use the documentation that came with the Windows NT or Windows 2000 server. Once that's done, however, you still need to establish a way to transfer files from UltraDev's local folder on your Macintosh client to UltraDev's remote folder on the Windows server. You have two choices: the File Transfer Protocol (FTP) or AppleTalk via a local network.

The FTP option is relatively simple to implement. Just make sure you know the Internet Protocol (IP) address for the Windows server and read "Defining Your Web Site" on page 18. While a bit faster than FTP, AppleTalk requires additional configuration of the Windows server and the Macintosh client. Depending on which server you're using, see this appendix's sections on "Adding File Services to a Windows 2000 Server" or "Adding File Services to a Windows 2000 Server."

You'll also need to set server permissions to share UltraDev's remote folder with the Macintosh. That's explained in "Sharing Server Files with the Macintosh." Finally, you'll need to activate the client-server connection using the Macintosh's TCP/IP and AppleTalk control panels, which is explained in "Completing the Macintosh Client Setup."

NOTE *You are not limited to using Windows' File Services for Macintosh. Thursby Software's DAVE and Mirimar's PC-MacLAN also offer ways to network Mac clients and Windows servers. However, Windows 2000 Server comes with Services for Macintosh at no extra charge, making it the logical no-extra-cost option.*

ADDING FILE SERVICES FOR MACINTOSH TO A WINDOWS 2000 SERVER

To share a Windows 2000 folder with a Macintosh via AppleTalk, you need to install the File Services for Macintosh components, part of a larger Services for Macintosh (SFM) package that comes with the Windows server software. Be sure to have the Windows 2000 Server CD that was used to originally install the server software handy.

1) Choose Start > Settings > Control Panel > Add/Remove Programs on the server.
The Add/Remove Programs dialog box opens.

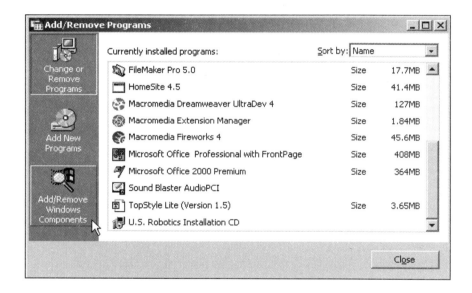

2) Click the Add/Remove Windows Components button.
It may take a moment before the Windows Components Wizard starts.

3) Scroll through the wizard's list of available components, select *Other Network File and Print Services*, and click the *Details* button.

270

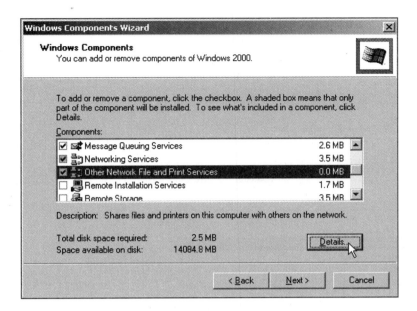

The Other Network File and Print Services dialog box appears, listing *File Services for Macintosh*, *Print Services for Macintosh*, and *Print Services for Unix*. While you only need the file services, you can select the second box if you want to make a networked PC laser printer available to any Macs on the network.

4) Check the *File Services for Macintosh* box and click *OK*.

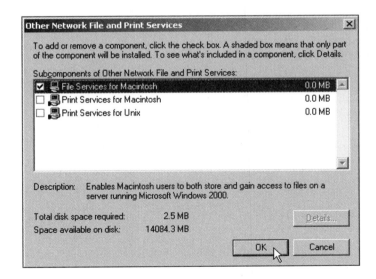

The Windows Components Wizard dialog box reappears.

5) Click *Next* to start the installation.

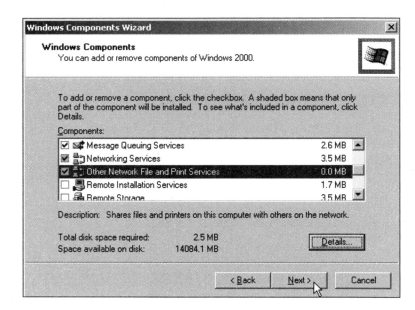

The wizard will install the necessary components and display a new dialog box when it's done.

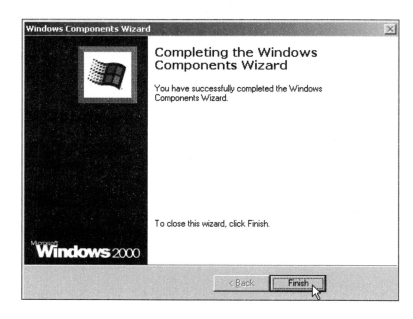

6) Click *Finish* and when the Add/Remove dialog box reappears, click *Close*.

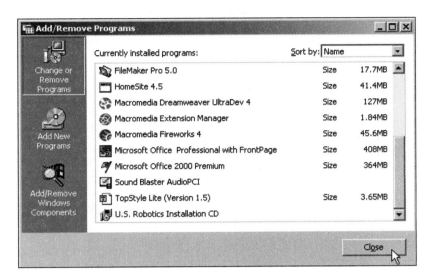

To set the server's file-sharing permissions to grant access to the Macintosh client, see "Sharing Windows 2000 Server Files with the Macintosh."

ADDING FILE SERVICES FOR MACINTOSH TO A WINDOWS NT SERVER

To share a Windows NT server folder with a Macintosh via AppleTalk, you need to install the File Services for Macintosh components, part of a larger Services for Macintosh (SFM) package that comes with the Windows server software. Be sure to have the Windows NT Server CD that was used to originally install the server software handy.

1) **Choose Start > Settings > Control Panel on the server. Double-click the *Network* icon.**
The Network Control panel appears.

2) **Click the *Services* tab, then click the *Add* button.**
The Select Network Service dialog box appears.

3) **Select *Services for Macintosh* in the list and click *OK* to start the installation.**
The *Services* tab reappears.

4) **Click *OK*.**
When asked to located the files needed for the installation, insert the NT Server CD.

5) Click *Continue*.

The Macintosh components will be installed, but you still need to configure the server to add the AppleTalk zone where your Mac client resides.

6) Select *Services for Macintosh* and click the *Properties* button.

The Services for Macintosh Properties dialog box will appear.

7) Click the *Routing* tab, check the *Enable Routing* and *Use This Router to Seed the Network* boxes.

The Network Ranges dialog box appears.

8) If you only have one AppleTalk zone, enter *1*. Otherwise, enter the appropriate number for the zone containing the UltraDev Mac client. Click *Add*, enter the exact name of the AppleTalk zone in the text field, and click *Add* again.

The name of the AppleTalk zone will be added to the list in the AppleTalk Protocol Properties dialog box. Repeat steps 7–8 until you've added all the zones containing UltraDev Mac clients.

9) Select the zone name you want the server to use as the default zone and click *Make Default*.

Close the dialog boxes to finish the procedure. To set the server's file-sharing permissions to grant access to the Macintosh client, see "Sharing Windows NT Server Files with the Macintosh."

SHARING WINDOWS 2000 SERVER FILES WITH THE MACINTOSH

Creating share privileges on the Windows server enables the Macintosh client machine to access the UltraDev files it needs. This procedure also lets you control the access rights of the users.

NOTE *Make sure the Microsoft Access database file,* andescoffee.mdb, *is copied to the* andes_extranet *folder so that it also will be covered by the permissions you've created.*

1) Choose Start > Settings > Control Panels > Administrative Tools > Computer Management.

The Computer Management dialog box opens.

2) Expand the *Shared Folders* list in the left-hand pane, right-click the *Shares* icon, and choose *New File Share*.

The Create Shared Folder dialog box will appear.

3) Click the *Browse* button to navigate to the folder you want to share, in this case C:\Inetpub\wwwroot\andes_extranet\.

NOTE *If you haven't already created the* andes_extranet *folder within the wwwroot folder, do so by clicking the New Folder button in the Browse For Folder dialog box.*

Once you navigate to the folder, click *OK* and the Create Shared Folder dialog box reappears.

4) Check *Apple Macintosh* in the *Accessible from the following clients* pane.

Microsoft Windows is checked by default. By checking both boxes, the same share name will be used for both systems.

5) Type *UltraDevExtranet* in the *Share name* text field.

The same name will appear automatically in the *Macintosh share name* text field. You can use whatever *Share name* works best for your organization's needs. Similarly, use the *Share description* text field to add any label that will help users distinguish this shared folder from others on the Windows server.

6) Click *Next* when you are done.

The Create Shared Folder dialog box will display a list of choices for setting permissions for what users can do with the folder's contents. By default, it is set to *All users have full control*. Unless only one or two people will be working on the site, however, it's best to create permissions customized for the members of your Web site team.

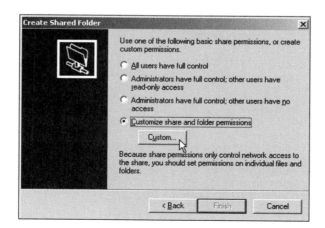

276

7) Choose *Customize share and folder permissions* and click the *Custom* button.

The Customize Permissions dialog box will open. Initially, the only *Name* listed will be *Everyone* with the *Permissions* set to allow all three possible actions.

8) Use the *Allow* and *Deny* checkboxes to limit the folder access offered to *Everyone*, then click the *Add* button to create individual user profiles with the appropriate permissions.

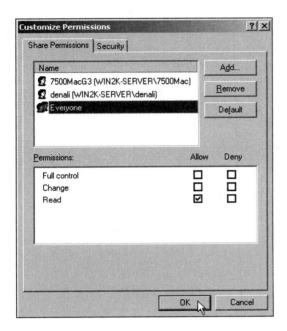

After creating the necessary *Names* and *Permissions* for your site, click *OK* to close the dialog box. The Create Shared Folder dialog box will reappear.

9) Click *Finish*.

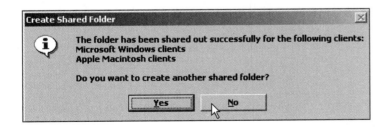

A dialog box will appear asking if you want to create another shared folder. If there are still more folders you want to share, click Yes. Otherwise click No and the Computer Management dialog box now will include a Macintosh and Windows version of the shared folder you just created.

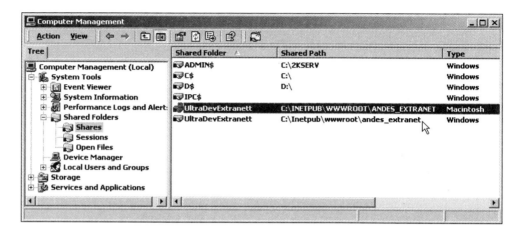

Before you can use the local network via AppleTalk, see "Completing the Macintosh Client Setup."

SHARING WINDOWS NT SERVER FILES WITH THE MACINTOSH

Creating share privileges on the Windows server enables the Macintosh client machine to access the UltraDev files it needs. This procedure also lets you control the access rights of the users.

NOTE *Make sure the Microsoft Access database file,* andescoffee.mdb, *is copied to the* andes_extranet *folder so that it also will be covered by the permissions you've created.*

1) Launch the File Manager and select in the left pane the folder you want to share, in this case C:\Inetpub\wwwroot\andes_extranet\. Choose MacFile > Create Volume.

The Create Macintosh Accessible Volume dialog box appears with the *Volume Name* and *Path* automatically set for the selected folder. By default, *Volume Security* is set to *Guests can use this volume.*

2) Uncheck the *Guests can use this volume* box and click the *Permissions* button.

The Macintosh View of Directory Permissions dialog box appears.

3) Set which users can *See Files*, *See Folders*, and *Make Changes*, then click *OK* to close the dialog box.

The Create Macintosh Accessible Volume dialog box reappears.

4) Click *OK* to close the dialog box.

Before you can use the local network via AppleTalk, however, you need to finish a couple of items in the Macintosh client setup.

COMPLETING THE MACINTOSH CLIENT SETUP

1) Choose Apple > Control Panels > TCP/IP.

The TCP/IP Control Panel opens.

2) Make sure the *Connect via* pop-up menu is set to *Ethernet*, then close the dialog box.

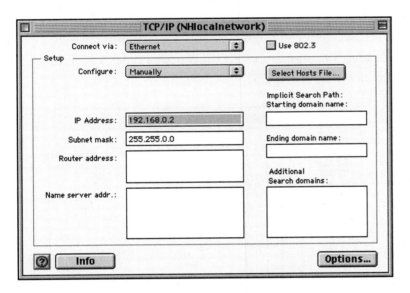

3) Choose Apple > Control Panels > AppleTalk.

The AppleTalk Control Panel opens.

279

4) Make sure the _Connect via_ pop-up menu is set to _Ethernet_, then close the dialog box.

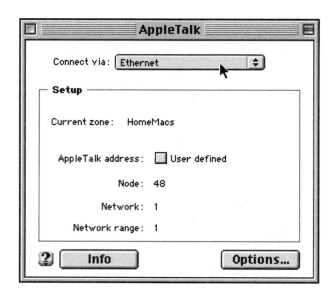

TIP _If you only have one AppleTalk zone, it already will be selected as the_ Current Zone.

5) Choose Apple > Chooser > Appleshare, select the Windows server's name in the right-hand list, and click _OK_.

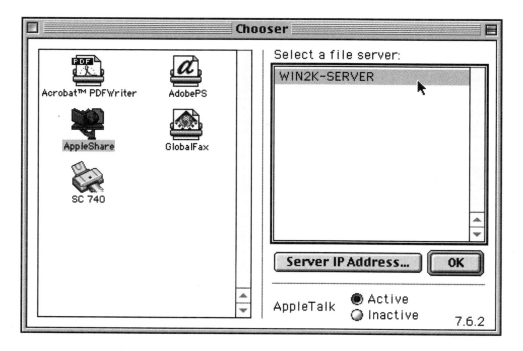

280

The Connect dialog box opens.

6) Select *Registered User*, enter the *Name* and *Password* that you previously set on the Windows server, and click *Connect*.

A dialog box opens, listing all the folders on the Windows server to which you've been granted share privileges.

7) Select the UltraDev extranet folder and click *OK*.

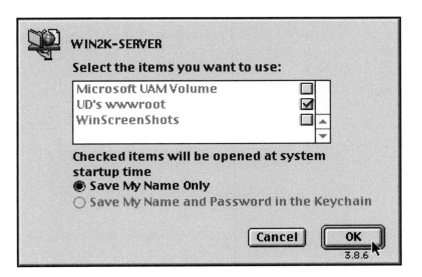

The UltraDev root folder will appear on the Macintosh desktop, enabling you to move files to it as needed. You're now ready to finish defining your Web site, as explained on page 18 of Lesson 2.

index

Learn Macromedia's hottest software...
the **Visual QuickStart** way!

Visual QuickStart Guides

Get Up and Running Fast. *Visual QuickStart Guides from Peachpit Press cover Macromedia software and are published in association with Macromedia Press. They are the industry's bestselling series of practical, visual, quick-reference guides. Step-by-step instructions and plenty of screen shots show you how to do the most important tasks and get right to work.*

macromedia®
PRESS

www.peachpit.com/mmp